SOME FAVOURITE BOOKS

SOME FAVOURITE BOOKS

John Macleod

THE BANNER OF TRUTH TRUST

THE BANNER OF TRUTH TRUST
3 Murrayfield Road, Edinburgh, EH 12 6EL
PO Box 621, Carlisle, Pennsylvania 17013, USA

★

First published in the *Monthly Record* of the Free Church of
Scotland, 1918–22.
© *The Banner of Truth 1988*
First Banner of Truth Edition 1988
ISBN 0 85151 538 X

★

Typeset in 10½/12pt Linotron Plantin
At The Spartan Press Limited, Lymington, Hants
Printed and bound in Great Britain by
Hazell Watson & Viney Limited,
Member of the BPCC Group,
Aylesbury, Bucks

Contents

Preface

Dr John Macleod (1872–1948) was well known in his day as a Christian leader in Scotland and beyond but he rarely appeared as an author. His only well-known volume was *Scottish Theology – In relation to Church History Since the Reformation*, (1943) reprinted jointly by the Knox Press (Edinburgh) and the Banner of Truth Trust in 1974.

In this book a valued series of articles which Dr Macleod wrote for the *Monthly Record* of the Free Church of Scotland between the years 1918 and 1922 has been brought together for the first time. These articles, which provide pen-pictures of authors and their major works, will give many readers an introduction to a whole series of books. It is a happy sign of our times that although many of these books were out of print when Macleod wrote, they are once again available. To possess them is to possess what others, as well as John Macleod, regard as among the best works to be found in English-speaking Christianity.

It needs to be borne in mind by the reader that when the author refers to the length of time which has passed since the events he records, he was himself speaking nearly seventy years ago.

The gratitude of the Publishers is expressed to Professor Douglas MacMillan and to the Free Church of Scotland to whom we are indebted for the availability of these pages. Footnotes have been added to the text by the present publishers.

1 : William Guthrie's *The Christian's Great Interest*

It was an old and a healthy tradition in Scotland that each home where the light of godliness shone should have its own bookshelf, and among its treasures few were held in so much esteem as *The Christian's Great Interest*, by William Guthrie of Fenwick.[1] So long as the religious interest determined the character of our people's reading, this book had scarcely a rival in popularity, and it is little wonder that this should be so. It commended itself to the Christian conscience of the country, and kept its place as a religious classic for generations. Where the old order still holds, this choice book is well known. And the more it is known the better, for a saner book in the things of the soul one can scarcely find.

ITS WRITER

The writer was born in 1620 and died in 1665. He was the eldest son of Guthrie of Pitforthie, near Brechin, and a near relative of James Guthrie of Stirling, the martyr of the Covenant. William Guthrie went to St Andrews to study, and there enjoyed the benefit of his cousin's company and tuition. But, what was more, he came under the power of the gospel through the ministry of holy Samuel Rutherford. When 'Christ's Prisoner at Aber-

[1] Ayrshire.

deen' was loosed, he was not left long in his loved Anwoth by the Solway. The Second Reformation[1] called him away from the seclusion of his country charge, and he was appointed Divinity Professor in our most ancient University.[2] The work of this post did not silence him as a preacher, and his preaching was not in vain. Should it have done nothing in the old city by the sea but call William Guthrie, its success was notable, for not even John Livingstone himself or David Dickson exercised a more blessed ministry in that great generation than did the minister of Fenwick.

At the age of twenty-four Guthrie was settled in his only charge, and he closed his public work twenty years later. About a year before his death he was silenced. His brethren had been outed two years before, but local feudal and baronial influence had been active on his behalf, and for these two years he was left undisturbed. In 1664, however, the Episcopal closure was applied, and his public witness came to an end. Some years earlier, notes of his sermons were published in a very imperfect form by others, and with a boastful title. In self-defence he felt compelled to put himself right with the public, and the result was the publication of *The Christian's Great Interest*.[3] It is the authentic monument of his labours. Those who are curious will find other sermons of his in print which were taken down by hearers. However good these are, they were not prepared by the author's hand for the press, nor meant to be on permanent record. His own work gives the marrow of his teaching, and with it one can come to an understanding of the type of godliness that prevailed in Scotland in the

[1]The writer of these reviews is fond of speaking of the second Reformation. In Scotland, this refers to the emancipation of the Presbyterian Church from Episcopalian interference by the National Covenant of 1638.
[2]St Andrews.
[3]1658. The book is still available from Banner of Truth.

days of the Covenants and the Commonwealth, and it lets us see the kind of doctrine that was most appreciated and the method employed by a master in Israel in dealing with his exercised and interested hearers.

ITS STYLE AND PURPOSE

The book makes no pretensions to style, yet attains, however, to what was not its aim. It is written as a practical work on such a theme should be, in a style that is plain and perspicuous, direct and homely, and alongside the excellence of its subject matter these qualities have contributed to its long-lived usefulness.

The Evangel had put its mark on the life of Scotland, and men were much in earnest about the question of what share they had themselves in the hopes that it warrants. They knew that eternal life is in Christ. What they sought to read was their own title to that life, and this they felt they could do only as they reached a personal certainty of their union with their Lord. The comfort of such an assurance they sought for themselves, and they noticed that they must go warily about the matter. Their religion was no mere window-dressing to conceal the emptiness and poverty that lay behind; and our sturdy fathers would not be put off the scent by the suggestion that in examining themselves they were pulling up the roots of their faith to see if it was growing. They were satisfied that a disinclination to try themselves by the standard of gospel truth is a feature of those with whom things are not in a good way. It savoured too much of the fraudulent bankrupt. So they prized teaching that gave their own place to the subjective realities of the kingdom of God. For men thus minded, Guthrie's book furnished the very guidance they needed, and so long as our countrymen will seek to make sure work of their salvation, they will value what their fathers valued.

ITS TWO PARTS

The first part of the book is taken up with the 'Trial of a Saving Interest in Christ.' Beginning, as good Protestant literature of its kind should do, with an assertion of the possibility that a believer should come to be satisfied that he is a child of God, it lays stress on the importance of reaching such a comfortable conclusion, and points out that the matter can be determined only by Scripture. It then discusses why so few arrive at this desirable knowledge, and it removes stumbling blocks out of the way. Then it goes on to treat of conviction of sin, saving or otherwise; faith; the new creature and the difference between the true Christian and the counterfeit; and in closing it clears up a variety of difficulties that timid believers feel in regard to fellowship with God. The second part of the work handles the practical question of how to attain to a saving interest in Christ, and it opens up the gospel way, answers objections and solves difficulties. The sin against the Holy Spirit is dealt with in a judicious way, and, after some further special objections are answered, the book concludes with a chapter on personal covenanting. The whole is a marvel of condensation and clearness, and the work is one of the immortals of evangelical theology.

2: The *Life* of Thomas Halyburton

A generation must arise in Evangelical Scotland that knows not Joseph before the memory of Thomas Halyburton is lost. The fragrance that clings to the name of the righteous is his. More than two hundred years have gone since he ran his race, and the names of the great and the mighty who cut a figure on the stage of public life as his contemporaries are most of them known now only to the curious. Yet such is the immortality given even on earth to outstanding godliness, that over the gulf of centuries those who share his hope can feel their heart warm at the mention of his name. There may still be some whose religious life has sprung from their acquaintance with his writings, just as long ago the touch of the bones of Elisha brought life to the dead. Yet it is to be feared that the circle of those that are familiar with Halyburton's memory is smaller in this cold and unbelieving age than in any of the intervening generations. Unless people take their religion seriously, and are willing to exercise themselves in the severe task of thinking out its problems, one need not expect that any great store will be set by him. For Thomas Halyburton was an intense thinker. Indeed, one of the most competent judges of such a matter, Dr Hugh Martin, has left on record his estimate of him as a theologian. This brackets him with William Cunningham as one of the two greatest theologians that our country ever produced. This is high praise, and it is worth while considering the work of such a man.

THE RELIGIOUS CONDITION OF HIS AGE

Like many of the brightest lights that our Church has seen, Halyburton finished his work on earth while he was yet young. Thus he is in the goodly fellowship of Andrew Gray, Hugh Binning, James Durham, William Dunlop, and Robert McCheyne. He was born in the year 1674, and in 1712 he died, in his thirty-eighth year. Thus his course, if bright, was brief. In his boyhood his widowed mother took him to Rotterdam to escape the persecution that raged in Scotland, but after the Revolution[1] Settlement, like his contemporaries, Thomas Boston and Robert Wodrow, he studied for the ministry of the gospel. Those were days of gladness to the Church which had weathered the storm. There was not only joy for deliverance from bondage and tyranny; in much of Scotland they were happy days of spiritual refreshing. James Wodrow, the father of the historian, was then Professor of Divinity in Glasgow. He lived in close fellowship with the Dunlops and the Stirlings of those days, as he had done with Donald Cargill of an earlier day. He gave it as his deliberate opinion that there was a richer outpouring of the Spirit after the Revolution than he had seen in the closing years of the Commonwealth. But with this revived Evangelism the Church had to bear a deadweight of neutral or negative conformity admitted into her ministry. Their influence fostered the tendency which in its later developments came to be known as Moderatism. Of the incipient progress of this evil thing, Halyburton before his death was well aware. The thing, as we say, was in the air. Infidelity had raised its head in Italy, even in Vatican circles, during the Renaissance; again in French Court

[1] The Revolution of 1688 which deposed the Roman Catholic James II and enthroned William of Orange and Mary.

circles in the seventeenth century. After the Restoration[1] it spread among the upper classes in England, and English Deism set the fashion for Western Europe. An unbelieving age had no place for the mysteries of gospel grace, and degenerate Nonconformists in England forsook the faith of their fathers, while many of the Conforming ministry on both sides of the Border looked on subscription to the Confession and Articles that set forth the faith of the Reformation as a yoke of bondage. A decay of spiritual life had set in, and such an attitude toward the faith blighted the life of the Church and of the nation, for godliness depends for its strength on the conviction with which the gospel is held and preached.

SOME OF HIS WRITINGS

Alongside the early growth of this unbelieving tendency was the revived preaching of the old gospel, and Halyburton in his life illustrated the working of both. In his religious exercises before his conversion, his vigorous mind grappled with unbelief in various phases, and when he came to the light of gospel freedom he did so as one well schooled in the controversy of the age. The monument of his literary life is his confutations of Deism.[2] It is one of the great books on the subject. It is the outcome of the mental and spiritual struggles through which he came to an assured confidence in the evangel, and the record of these struggles we have in his *Life*. Halyburton was settled as minister of Ceres, in Fife, in May, 1700, and the sermon is published which he preached on his first Sabbath with his people. A more suitable text for an inaugural discourse could scarcely be found (*Acts 10. 29*), 'I ask therefore,

[1]The Restoration of the Stuarts in the person of Charles II, 1660.
[2]*Natural Religion Insufficient and Revealed necessary to Man's Happiness.* 1714 (all Halyburton's Works were published posthumously).

for what intent ye have sent for me?' And as the theme is appropriate, the treatment is worthy of his early powers. Shortly after the Disruption of 1643 the like-minded John Donaldson was settled as the first Free Church minister of Ceres, and in connection with his settlement this discourse of his great predecessor was republished, with a short introduction from the pen of Dr John Duncan. Dr Duncan was a great admirer of Halyburton. He classed him with Hermann Witsius as one of the school of Owen in the Reformed Theology, though he did not rank either of them quite as high as their master. As fruits of his work in the ministry, we have the series of sermons that he preached – six Communion sermons and 'The Great Concern of Salvation.' This latter is one of the best and most useful practical works among our noteworthy Evangelical classics.

A GREAT SPIRITUAL BIOGRAPHY

Though far from being finished as a piece of bookcraft, the *Life of Halyburton* is the presentation of the progress of a powerful mind from darkness to light, and it holds a high place among the great works of spiritual biography. That master of experimental theology, Archibald Alexander of Princeton, refers to Halyburton's account of the change he had undergone as one of the most satisfactory things in the whole range of Christian biography. 'I have not met,' says he, 'with any account of Christian experience which is so full and satisfactory as this, and when it is known to have been written by a man of sound understanding and most exemplary piety . . . when his judgment was matured by much experience, it cannot but furnish a decisive proof of the reality of experimental religion which cannot be gainsaid. In these exercises there is not a tincture of enthusiasm . . . We see also how high the exercises of scriptural piety may rise without degenerating into any extravagance.'

But the work that gives us the man himself, with all his struggles and all his comfort in the gospel salvation, is his *Life*. Few more affecting or triumphant things can be found than the narrative of his deathbed. This *Life* was one of the works which preserved the salt of Evangelical teaching and witness in the eighteenth century. When one turns to the life of that remarkable Christian, Sir Richard Hill, Rowland Hill's elder brother, one finds how useful this biography was to him at the outset of his new life, and how highly esteemed it was also by Fletcher of Madeley. After a ministry of ten years at Ceres, Halyburton became Professor of Theology at St Andrews. Here, however, he did not labour long. His infirm health settled down into decline. He lies buried near Samuel Rutherford and other worthies, such as Forrester and Anderson – 'a knot of comely dust,' as he puts it – and the spot where these saints sleep has been the resort for meditation of godly folk whose minds drew them more to the worthies of the past than to the men among whom they lived and moved. We trust that the place of honour long held among our pious and intelligent people of *Halyburton's Life* will long continue to be given to it, and that it may be among our households a favourite book.

HIS TESTIMONY TO HIS DOCTOR

'Doctor, as to this piece of work, you are near an end with it. I wish you may lay it to heart – it will come to your door, too; and it is a business of great moment to die like a Christian, and it is a rarity . . . I wish the Lord Himself may show you kindness. The greatest kindness I am now capable of showing you is to commend serious religion to you. There is a reality in religion, doctor; this is an age that has lost the sense of it . . . I bless God, I was educated by godly parents in the principles of the Church of Scotland; I bless Him that when I came to riper years, I did on mature deliberation make them my choice; I bless the Lord, I have been helped ever since to adhere to them without wavering; I bless Him, I have seen that holiness yields peace and comfort in prosperity and adversity. What should I seek more to give evidence of the reality of it? . . . Now get acquaintance with God. The little acquaintance I have had with God within these two days has been better than ten thousand times the pains I have been at all my life about religion. It is good to have Him to go to when we are turning our face to the wall.'

COUNSEL TO HIS BROTHER-MINISTERS

'Now, brethren, give diligence; for the Lord's sake, ply your work; hold fast what you have. I must have a word to my brethren – it is on my heart. I am young, but I am near the end of my life, and that makes me old. It becomes me to take advice from you. However, it is only to exhort to diligence in the common salvation. I repent I did not more; but I have peace in it, that what I did, I did it in sincerity. He accepts of the mite. It was the delight of my heart to preach the Gospel, and it made me sometimes neglect a frail body. I ever thought if I could contribute to the saving of a soul, it would be a star, a crown, and a glorious crown. I know this was the thing I aimed at. I desired to decrease that the Bridegroom might increase.'

DELIVERANCE FROM THE FEAR OF DEATH

'God has shed abroad His love in my heart; and I am waiting for His salvation. Here is a demonstration of the reality of religion, that I, a poor, weak, timorous man, as much once afraid of death as any – I that have been many years under the terrors of death – come now in the mercy of God and by the power of His grace composedly, and with joy, to look death in the face. I have seen it in its paleness, and all the circumstances of horror attending it; I dare look it in the face in its most ghastly shape, and hope within a little to have the victory . . . You may believe a man venturing on eternity. I am not acting as a fool, but I have weighed eternity this last night. I have looked on death as stripped of all that is pleasant to nature; I have considered the spade and grave, and every circumstance in it that is terrible to nature; and under the view of all these, I have that in the way of God that gave satisfaction; not only a rational satisfaction, but a heart-engaging power attending it, that makes me rejoice.'

HIS BEST PULPIT AND TRIUMPHANT END

'Come, and see your friend in the best case that you ever saw him in – longing for a deliverance and "hastening to the coming of the day of God"; "waiting for the salvation of God", on a bed of roses, though nature and skin may not say so – a bed perfumed. And, man, I sent for you; I longed to see you, that I might give you encouragement in an ill world to preach the Gospel, and stand by Christ, that has been so good to me. This is the best pulpit that ever I was in. I am now laid on this bed for this end, that I may commend my Lord.

'All these soft clothes are like sacking about me, and yet I have perfect ease of spirit. My breast is drawing together as sorely as if it were with cords, and still the Lord keeps composure. What is this! I could have scarcely believed though I had been told it, that I could have kept in the right exercise of my judgment under this racking pain. Whatever come of it I am sure I am a demonstration that there is a reality in religion; and I rejoice in this, that God has honoured a sinful worm to be a demonstration of His grace . . . Worthy is the Lamb to receive glory.

'I was just thinking on the pleasant spot of earth that I will get to lie in, beside Mr Rutherford, Mr Forrester,[1] and Principal Anderson. And I will come in as the little one among them, and I will get my pleasant George[2] in my hand; and O, we will be a knot of bonnie dust.'

[1] Thomas Forrester (d.1706). Principal at St Andrew's College from 1698.

[2] Halyburton's son George died only a little time before his father.

3: The *Letters* of Samuel Rutherford

The life of Samuel Rutherford was lived in great days. Born in 1600, he died in 1661. In 1627 he became minister of Anwoth by the Solway. A modified Episcopacy had been forced on Scotland by its kings. But, like Baal of old, the bishop of Galloway must have been asleep or on a journey when Rutherford was settled at Anwoth without having to come under any engagements to comply with Episcopal innovations. For nine years he laboured in this quiet charge. His people came to know him as one who was always at his post, preaching or studying, visiting and catechising. His profiting appeared. His whole heart was in his ministry, and the closeness of his walk with God showed itself in his public work. His church was crowded by serious Christians, not only from the country within easy reach, but from a distance too. Some of John Welsh's old hearers from Ayr might be found, in this hunger for heavenly food, going as far as Anwoth to wait upon the preaching of the Word. But all the notable success of his early ministry would not have made his name the household word which it came to be. The alabaster box of that ministry must be broken that its fragrance might be diffused, and things came to the breaking-point in 1636.

BANISHED TO ABERDEEN

In that year he published in Holland a Latin work in defence of the doctrines of Grace and so took part in the

Arminian Controversy. This gave offence to the bishop, who, as one of the school of Laud, took the Arminian side. Until after the Synod of Dort (1619) the prelatic Conformists in Scotland were Augustinian in their teaching. Indeed, in 1616 they drew up an orthodox Confession of Faith, and even afterwards neither John Forbes of Carse nor William Guild nor Robert Leighton could be spoken of as Arminian. Sydserff, bishop of Galloway, however, was sufficiently plastic to conform to Court fashion, and once the star of Laud was in the ascendancy royal patronage was extended to the Arminians. So evident was this that soon the question, 'What do the Arminians hold?' admitted of the answer that they held the best bishoprics and deaneries in England. It was not fashionable then to enter the lists against what was for the time being 'the New Theology.' Rutherford was called before the High Commission Court. Episcopacy had adopted the five articles of Perth[1] which innovated on the worship of the Reformed Church, and in regard to them Rutherford was a Nonconformist. Such a dangerous man must be banished, and banished he accordingly was. Thus was the alabaster box broken.

PATMOS BECOMES A PISGAH

His place of exile was Aberdeen, which had as many universities as the whole of England and was the headquarters of the Conforming party in Scotland. The primate might have his seat at St Andrews, but the leaven of Erastian[2] truckling to the Royal Supremacy had wrought

[1] Passed in 1618 in the attempt to shackle Presbyterianism and introduce Episcopacy. The most obnoxious to Presbyterians prescribed kneeling to receive 'the communion' and submission to bishops. King James was pressing hard for these innovations.

[2] Thomas Erastus (d. 1583) was a Swiss physician who denied the right of the church to exercise discipline. Most of his followers taught that the church should be subordinate to the state.

more powerfully in and about Aberdeen than anywhere else in the land. Present-day Moderatism recognises its spiritual kinship with the Aberdeen Doctors who opposed the Covenant of 1638, and Moderatism has all along been in closer sympathy with royal claims than with Christian freedom. The place, then, of Rutherford's exile was where he was least likely to find sympathy with himself or with his principles. But for all the coldness of Northern love his Patmos became a Pisgah, and the letters that he wrote his favourite friends as Christ's prisoner in Aberdeen speak the high and holy fellowship that he enjoyed with his exalted Lord. They preserve the savour of that ministry which Church tyranny had cut short. Of the 365 letters given in Bonar's Edition, 220 were written during the eighteen months of his stay in Aberdeen. Of these many were written on the same day, so overflowing was the anointing that the writer enjoyed. Such as it was we should be thankful for the efficiency of the postal arrangements of the day, for the letters reached their destination. Those who got them prized them as treasures and preserved them, and so we have them still as a refreshing for the Church of God in other days and even to the ends of the earth.

The Second Reformation[1] movement set the captive free. He was not long left at Anwoth. Appointed to a Divinity Chair at St Andrews, he became principal of the New College there. In the stirring times of the Westminster Assembly and the Commonwealth he took his full share of public work. When a rift came in the lute and brethren saw no longer eye to eye he stood out as a Protester who would not budge an inch. Such a man could scarcely escape the martyr's crown when Charles II was restored. Things were in train to bring him before the

[1]See footnote 1 (Ch.1 p.8).

king's courts, but the King of kings intervened, and holy Rutherford was called to the courts above, where 'glory, glory dwelleth in Immanuel's land.'

QUALITY OF THE LETTERS

'The sands of time are sinking,' a cento of choice expressions of his culled not only from his letters but from his other works, gives us a speaking picture of his heavenly exercise. There was a luxuriance about his thought that was almost Oriental in its profusion, and his gift of expression gave suitable utterance to it. The love of Christ had taken him captive, and his mind was estimated with the language in which the Word of God gives expression to the deep affections of the heart. Fault has been found with the erotic character of his language, but one must plough with his heifer to read his riddle, and the false prudery that takes exception to the rich and free utterance that he gives to the love of the soul does not shrink from reflecting upon the Word from which he drew his speech. Rutherford, the man, the scholar, the saint, the divine, is one of our most precious names. He wrote much, but of all his works that which has outdistanced the rest is the collection of his letters. To this collection, when it first appeared, the quaint name of *Joshua Redivivus* was given by his faithful disciple and friend, Robert Macward.[1] The name means Joshua alive again. Joshua brought back a good report of the Land of Promise with the grapes of Eshcol. He was honoured to lead the Church of the wilderness into that land. He was strong and courageous, and as for him and his house he was resolved to serve the Lord. The name was not ill-bestowed. For few have ever given a better report of his

---

[1] A covenanting minister who died at Rotterdam in 1687.

Lord and of His land than did the godly Rutherford. And few have been more honoured than he in bringing, by way of foretaste, his fellow-pilgrims into the good of the everlasting heritage of the saints. Few also have so fully and unreservedly served and followed the Lord. Macward when he published the letters was an exile for the witness of the Church of Scotland, Reformed and then in the furnace. It is most likely that the letters were first printed and published in the land of the editor's exile. The first two editions conceal their place of origin. These were evil days for the good cause and it was not always advisable that tyrants should know where the books of our worthies were prepared for circulation. The security afforded to Macward and his fellow-exiles in the Netherlands awakened the jealousy of their persecutors at home who made endeavours to interfere with their right of sanctuary. Since ever they saw the light these letters have been held in the highest esteem by the godly, and possibly there is no religious work of Scottish authorship that has circulated so widely and has so strongly influenced the heart of the Church at large.[1]

[1]The *Letters* (edited by Andrew A. Bonar) are obtainable in a Banner of Truth reprint.

4: James Durham on *Isaiah*

'Read Durham on the 53rd of Isaiah' was the advice of Dr John Duncan; 'it is eating the flesh and drinking the blood of the Son of God.' This surely is a high encomium to pass on any book. The work referred to is a series of sermons on the great Messianic chapter. In olden days our good ministers were wont to preach 'on their ordinary,' which might mean that a single text was taken up and exhaustively handled in a number of successive sermons, or a series of sermons was delivered on a continuous portion of Scripture. We have a monument of the preaching of the golden age of the seventeenth century pulpit in this volume from the pen of the judicious Durham.

'THE JUDICIOUS' DURHAM

If an earlier generation of the Church of England boasted of a judicious Hooker, our own Church and country were not behind. The works of James Durham show with what good judgment the name 'judicious' was given him. Hooker handled, in the main, questions of an ecclesiastical kind. He is the representative Elizabethan champion of the Anglican Reformation settlement. As such he is as strenuous in his opposition to Puritanism as he is powerful in his treatment of other questions. He has left his name as that of one of the foremost of English theological writers. But our own Durham, without devoting himself to the defence of the Puritanism which he represented, gives a splendid specimen of good judgment applied to the evangelical verities which lie at the very core of the Church's life. The contrast between these judicious divines is characteristic of the difference between the polemic and controversial character of much of the classical divinity of England and the practical and experimental character of most of the standard theology of Scotland. The one kind dealt with such questions as exercise the wit of the schools; the other with those that touch the heart and conscience of the believer and the Church of God.

HIS SPHERE OF LABOUR

James Durham was one of the galaxy of stars that shone in our Church's firmament about the middle of the seventeenth century. In the wars of the Second Reformation[1] he was a captain, as might well be looked for in a grave young laird from Angus who was not ashamed of the cause of his Church or his covenanted country. Though brought up a Conformist with royal policy, he was led under the influence of his godly young wife to incline towards the evangel, and came powerfully under its sway. He prayed before battle at the head of his men one day, and that prayer drew the attention of a passer-by. This was none less than David Dickson of Irvine and Glasgow, who was then at the height of his influence in Scotland. He remitted the young captain for the service of the Gospel ministry. Soon his studies were completed, and Durham, at an early age, became a minister in Glasgow. He died before he was thirty-six. So his course, if bright, was brief. Those were the days when the preaching of the Word flourished in Glasgow and Glasgow flourished by the

[1]See footnote I (Ch.I p.8)

preaching of the Word. One has only to recall the names of the men associated during his ministry with that city and its neighbourhood to see what a favoured place it was. There were to be found David Dickson and Robert Baillie, Hugh Binning and Andrew Gray, John Carstares and Donald Cargill. If the westland became the seat and home of strong Whiggism, as that word was understood in the seventeenth century,[1] it was not without good reason, for some of our choicest worthies ministered there. And men who preached the Gospel of Christ with the Holy Ghost sent down from heaven left their mark on the country and on their generation.

HIS TIMES

These times were troublous if they were glorious. During the years of the Commonwealth, when the Church was rent in twain with the contendings of Resolutioners and Protesters, it tells of the sanity of Durham's judgment, and the evenness[2] of his walk, and the reputation he had

[1]The term 'whig' originated in the second half of the seventeenth century as a term of abuse. In Ayrshire the word was used of the sour milk formed when milk was lappered (curdled). The King's party in Scotland meant by 'whig' the Presbyterians (covenanters) who were in opposition to the King's policy.

[2]During the Civil War in the reign of Charles I, English Parliamentarians and Scots, at first united against the King, fell apart. English armies overcame and captured the King, who died upon the scaffold in 1649. England then became a Commonwealth. A Scottish Parliament, however, accepted Prince Charles (later Charles II) as their King. On his part, Charles very reluctantly and insincerely accepted the condition that he must adhere to the Scottish National Covenant and impose Presbyterianism throughout Great Britain and Northern Ireland. Swallowing the bitter pill, he thereupon landed in Scotland. The English Parliament then declared war on Scotland and Oliver Cromwell invaded Scotland, routing the Scots at Dunbar. About 4000 Scots were slain in the battle, 10,000 were taken prisoner – 'and this at the cost of less than 30 English lives'. It was a shattering blow for the Scottish Parliament and split their ranks. One party argued that their military defeat was to be accounted for by ungodliness in high places and required Charles

made, that the warring factions of the Synod which met apart, each chose him as their Moderator. The nomination he would accept only if they met together, and they did. Some of his fellows in Glasgow were strong Resolutioners like Robert Baillie: others, such as Binning and Patrick Gillespie, were strong Protesters. But both parties agreed in their estimate of the judgment of James Durham. Along with Dickson he is credited with being joint author of the *Sum of Saving Knowledge* which we usually find bound up with our Confession. Those who remember what McCheyne owed to this work will not lightly esteem it.

HIS CHARACTER

Durham's neighbour for a year or two during his short ministry was Mr Andrew Gray. If the course of Durham was short, Gray's was shorter still. And as these things ever must be that folk will have their preferences, the people showed a preference for the preaching of the younger man by thronging his church. This, however, so far from awakening jealousy in Durham's bosom gave him

---

to supply full proof of his adherence to the National Covenant. Another party condemned this policy. The first party was known as the Protesters, the second as the Resolutioners. Charles, with a hastily recruited army marched into England, pursued by Cromwell, who defeated the Scottish King in what he described as his 'crowning mercy'. Shortly Scotland was united to England and was represented in the English Parliament. But the rift between Protesters and Resolutioners persisted for some time.

(As a sequel to the above, it deserves mention that Cromwell, when in Scotland, is said to have attended on a particular Lord's Day a Presbyterian service *incognito* without any prior knowledge of the preacher on the occasion. As he left he is reputed to have said, 'I perceive (the preacher) to be a very great man, and in my opinion he might be chaplain to any prince in Europe, though I have never seen him nor heard him before'. The preacher was James Durham, a little under 30 years of age at the time.)

the opportunity of showing his self-denial and his joy that Christ was being preached. He was a staid, solid man whose steady-going studious spirit was not easily upset. He had not the cheerful versatility of his friend, Guthrie of Fenwick. Once they spent an evening together and Mr Guthrie indulged freely his vein of pleasantry. Then at worship he was called upon to pray. This he did with great liberty and holy familiarity. Ere they parted, the grave Durham said to his friend: 'Oh, William, you are a happy man. If I had been as merry as you have been I could not have been in such a serious frame for prayer for the space of forty-eight hours.' Each of these worthy men was after his kind. There are varieties of disposition and temperament; and what is natural and spontaneous in one may be altogether alien to another. The solemn and sweetly serious saint had his own experience of spiritual trial, and when at the age of thirty-five he lay on his deathbed he had his own share of it. His colleague in the Inner High Church of Glasgow was John Carstares. The worthy men lived on most brotherly terms. Their wives were sisters, the daughters of Mure of Glanderston, an elect household. Carstares came in to see his dying colleague and heard from him how his mind was at work. 'Brother,' said Durham, 'for all that I have preached or written there is but one Scripture I can remember or dare grip unto, tell me if I dare lay the weight of my salvation upon it – Whosoever cometh unto Me I will in no wise cast out.' Carstares answered, 'You may depend upon it though you had a thousand salvations at hazard.' Before long the cloud was scattered, and Durham died in triumph.

HIS WORKS

Most of Durham's works saw the light after his death, edited by his widow and Carstares. They comprise his

Commentary on the Revelation, his *Exposition of the Song of Songs*[1], his work on *The Ten Commandments*, a series of sermons on the Unsearchable Riches of Christ, and his *Treatise on Scandal* or the treatment of offences and stumbling-blocks in the Church of God. About a hundred years after his death a short lecture exposition on the Book of Job appeared along with a few sermons. This piece is very rare. Mr Spurgeon, when he compiled a list of commentaries on Scripture and its books, failed to come upon a copy of it, though he knew of its existence. Our great Scottish work on this book, however, is that of his age-fellow, George Hutcheson of Edinburgh, who was a prince of expositors. There are also a few fugitive sermons of Durham's that have been published at various times. Most of his books have been repeatedly reprinted, even his large work on the Revelation. But the most modern reprint of any of his productions is the edition of the exposition of the Song from the press of that publisher of Evangelical Classics, King, of Aberdeen, and edited by Gavin Parker, one of our godly Disruption worthies. The work on *The Ten Commandments* is a singularly judicious performance; and if Chalmers called the exposition of the Commandments given in our Larger Catechism, 'sanctification broken small,' we can scarely find such a guide to practice, a 'Ductor dubitantium,'[2] a handbook of sound casuistry, as this book affords. One has only to read his handling of the Fourth Commandment to see how the various questions that have in recent times been raised in regard to it were discussed in the seventeenth century, and that our historical Scottish teaching as to the observance of the Lord's Day did not take root in the faith of our fathers in any ignorance of what can be said against it. The *Commentary on the Revelation* gives what, in past days, was

[1]Republished by The Banner of Truth.
[2]'A guide to those in doubt'.

the accepted Protestant view of that book, and the work on *Scandal*, which Carstares published the year after Durham's death, was but an expansion of what he handles in discussing some of the Epistles to the Seven Churches. This has, ever since it appeared, been the classic work in our Theology dealing with its subject; and as it was called forth by the breach between Resolutioners and Protesters, it aimed at healing breaches, and is distinguished by its irenic quality and for the well-balanced proportion in which it gives the truth of God's Word bearing on the matter it treats of. Currie of Kinglassie in criticising the Seceders, and Wilson of Perth in defending the Secession,[1] both defer to Durham, and in later days Dr Begg on the one hand, and Dr Rainy on the other, alike referred to this work as setting forth the principles that should be recognised as regulative in the handling of questions bearing on Church Unions.

Durham on *The Song of Solomon* has long been looked upon as the standard Scottish work on the subject. It is rich in its statements of experimental godliness; but none of his works, of varied excellence though they be, excels the sermons that he preached on the 53rd of Isaiah. He there opens up the truth of the sacrifice and the intercession of our Lord, and in connection therewith the duties of preachers and hearers of the gospel, together with the diversified exercises of heart and soul that gospel truth is fitted to call forth. The more the reader of Durham has been tried in regard to these things, the more will he find in his rich pages that which is fitted to be helpful to him. And as judgment, balance, sanity was the leading feature of the writer's natural equipment, the judiciousness for which he was famed comes out nowhere with greater evidence than in his handling of those gospel truths in

[1] i.e. in the 1730's.

the knowledge and faith of which the life of the soul stands.

One will now have to hunt out old books to get the writings of James Durham, yet until the close of the eighteenth century they were part of the regular output of Scottish presses that printed the works of our old divines. And lovers of the sound teaching of our Covenanting worthies will not be hindered from searching after their treasures by the antiquated printing and spelling and the poor paper and binding they find in the well-thumbed volumes that formed the solid Sabbath reading of our fathers.

5: Thomas Boston's *Fourfold State*

If there is one book that more than any other stands out as representative of the best of our Scottish religious classics it is *Human Nature in its Fourfold State*. When George Macdonald wished to show his animus against the evangelical orthodoxy which had environed his earlier years and from which he had revolted, he makes his hero hide this book in his fiddle case. This is action quite in keeping with the Broad School outlook. That school claims breadth and denounces narrowness. But if breadth were taken to mean such thought as embraces the breadth of God's law and of His kingly thoughts of mercy, Broad Churchmen could make good no claim to it. They would rank as narrow, and those that they would banish from the memory of their fellows would be acknowledged to be truly broad. A broad man in this good sense Thomas Boston was. And among his fellows he was a prince. Few men have ever been better versed in the religious literature of Scotland than the first and the great Thomas M'Crie, and he has left on record that, in his opinion, this work of his fellow townsman is the most useful and influential that has ever appeared in our country, for the book met with such acceptance from the godly throughout the land.

THE WRITER

Thomas Boston's life is as well known as that of any of our worthies. His autobiography lets us see who he was and how he passed through life. This work has seen various editions. Indeed, in the last quarter of a century no fewer than three editions of it have seen the light. It is the life of one who was out-and-out a Christian and a minister, grave, studious, and upright. Thomas Boston's picture is a living one in the gallery of our saints and scholars. He was born in 1676 and died in 1732. In his boyhood he came under powerful gospel impressions through the preaching of Henry Erskine, whose two sons, Ebenezer and Ralph, were to be his fellows in later years in the line they took to set forth the truth of the gospel. Later, after his college years, he came in touch with the north-country worthy and confessor James Fraser of Brea, who, after the Revolution, became minister of Culross. After a noviciate at Simprin he became in 1707 minister of Ettrick,[1] where he ended his work on earth.

HIS TEACHING

At the outset of his ministry Boston lighted upon a book whose method and outlook were destined profoundly to influence his life and teaching. This was *The Marrow of Modern Divinity*. It dated from the days of the Westminster Assembly, and when its title spoke of 'Modern Divinity' it referred to that which was modern in the maturity of the Puritan movement. The method of dealing with law and gospel which he found in this work proved to be very helpful to him. It cleared his mind as to the freeness of gospel grace and the ample warrant that every sinner who hears the gospel has to avail himself of its gracious provision. Gospel preaching had in some circles in Evangelical Scotland come to be very much an

[1] Ettrick on Ettrick water, is in S. Selkirkshire, about 18 miles S.W. of Selkirk. Simprin is a small parish 'down in the Merse about 5 miles east of Duns'.

exhibition of experimental case divinity. As the result of
this there was a hesitancy to preach freely and without
qualifications and reservations the good news to all sinners
of a Saviour who lives to receive as many as are willing to
betake themselves to Him. Boston found the teaching of
The Marrow in this matter good for himself alike as a man
and as a minister. He felt that it enabled him to bring
gospel appeals home to his hearers and to shut them up to
the obedience of faith. For his approval of *The Marrow* he
had to stand fire. It was reprinted by his friend James
Hogg of Carnock, the nephew of the apostolic Thomas
Hogg of Kiltearn, and its friends had to play the man in its
defence.

'THE MARROW CONTROVERSY'

At times we come across accounts of what is called the
'Marrow Controversy,' which would make it appear that
the opposition which the teaching of Fisher's book met
was due altogether to incipient Moderatism. There is little
doubt that the modified Calvinism of Richard Baxter
influenced very materially the thinking of many of our
Scottish preachers and it paved the way for the light, or in
modern phrase, the ethical, type of doctrine that became
the recognised teaching of the 'Moderate' party in the
eighteenth century. It is no doubt also true that 'Marrow'
teaching runs directly in the teeth of this tendency. Thus
so far as Baxter's influence was at work among the divines
of the Church of Scotland it would bring them into conflict
with the unfettered gospel of 'The Marrow.' But it is quite
an unfair statement of the case to represent Blackwell of
Paisley and afterwards of Aberdeen, Allan Logan of
Culross, Robert Wodrow, Dunlop, or even Principal
Hadow, as men who were unevangelical in their tendency.
And some of these were among the leaders of the

Assembly which condemned 'the Marrow.' In espousing the cause of the book which had been the means of such good to himself, Boston, whose name is with the Laodiceans a byword for rigid orthodoxy, was by the Erskines and the other Marrow men suspected of being an innovator. The Assembly condemned the book, and no doubt there were in its pages expressions which laid it open to censure. But Boston set to the task of preparing a new edition with notes, and whatever value attaches to the composite volume is found particularly in the notes of the pastor of Ettrick.

A FIGHT FOR THE FAITH

Something worse than the questionable orthodoxy of Baxter had begun to raise its head in the Church of Scotland. And the cases against Simson of Glasgow show how far the leaven of what afterwards came to be known as Moderatism was already at work. Moderatism has always been and must ever, in keeping with its genius, be a veiled unbelief. At times the veil is down. At times it is lifted. But unbelief is at the heart of the thing. We hear of the 'dark days of Moderatism' – and they were dark indeed. But some men speak of them and fail to see that the self-same leaven which made Moderatism what it was is at work in the twentieth century as surely as it was in the eighteenth. And its work is all the more successful that its true nature is not seen. In the fight for the faith that the orthodox had to put up they had to defend the cardinal truth of the real Godhead of our Lord and Saviour. Our present-day Moderatism, as represented by such a man as the late Dr Denney, is as much at sea on this subject as ever Simson of Glasgow was. But a generation destitute of theological discernment or lacking zeal and courage to stand for the truth will let the cloudy teaching of their contemporaries pass without challenge, while that same teaching hides from the Church's eyes the splendour of the firmament which sets forth the glory of God's unspeakable gift. When, as a member of the Assembly, Boston was personally dissatisfied with a finding reached in this business, he stood alone in dissenting from it. It is to this that his friend and yokefellow, Ralph Erskine, refers in his elegy.

> The great, the grave, judicious Boston's gone,
> Who once like Athanasius stood alone.

WORK AND WORKS

In his upland parish Boston met with his difficulties, and not the least trying of these were due to the Separatist policy of those that sympathised with the Cameronian extremists. But though some of his own parishioners failed to discern the gift of the ascended Lord, who was at work among them, there were exercised souls from other parts who made their way to Ettrick. Tradition tells of some that walked forty miles to wait upon his ministry. The sincere and upright work of a man of God does not often pass without tokens of success, and such tokens attested and crowned Boston's labours, and the memory of them has been handed down to later days. In his own life-time, so isolated were the different parts of the country owing to defective means of communication, that his contemporary, Robert Wodrow, speaking of him in a letter, seems to refer to him as though he was a man little known. Now that time has elapsed, we can look back to those days and wonder how it could be that the man who bulks largest in our view in his generation should be obscure in any part of evangelical Scotland while he lived. But the sermons that were preached with such prayer and pains in Ettrick came to be known elsewhere, and the series that makes up the *Fourfold State* was published in Edinburgh and it soon found a public. This it has retained ever since. There are few works 200 years old that are now in print, but the fact that there is still a demand for this one shows its vitality. In the Evangelical revival a Gaelic translation of it did great good in the Highlands, and the existence of the Free Church as a gospel force in some districts is largely due to the acceptance that this work met with among our godly forbears.

The collected writings of Thomas Boston – apart from his Latin works on the Hebrew points – are in twelve volumes in Macmillan's edition. They comprise his work on the Covenants, an exposition of the Shorter Catechism, his miscellany questions, and various sermons. But the work by which his name lives is the *Fourfold State*. We should wish that the Sabbath reading of our homes would continue to be in the good solid writers of the past, and where in any case this has ceased to be so, there should be a return to the old ways. Boston was a plain man, who wrote without pretence or ostentation, but one can read few serious writers whose style is so pleasing for its simplicity and its lucid clearness. And a better handbook of sound theology one can hardly find than what is supplied by this masterpiece.[1]

[1]Boston's *Memoirs*, widely recognised as one of the choicest reformed autobiographies has also been reprinted by the Banner of Truth.

6: The *Writings* of John Love

From early years we have been acquainted with the name Lovedale. This mission school is near the town of Alice in Cape Colony. It owes its name to John Love, of whose writings we propose to say a little. In the history of missionary effort about the end of the eighteenth and the beginning of the nineteenth century few names hold a more honoured place than his. He was one of the original Secretaries of the London Missionary Society, and after he returned to Scotland he was one of the mainstays of the Glasgow Missionary Society. And the station of Lovedale has been called after him in a portion of the mission field which this Society cultivated.

HIS EARLY LIFE AND ITS MEMORIALS

Dr Love was born in Paisley in the year 1757 and studied at the University of Glasgow, which he entered at a very early age. In his youth he was in danger of becoming a Socinian – for a tendency in the direction of that negation of the Christian faith known as Socinianism[1] was then strongly at work in Scotland. It was at work also beyond the Border, and Theophilus Lindsey avowed his Socinian sentiments and was so far honest as to leave the ministry of the Church of England. But the Socinianising tenor that wrought in Scotland was of a less reputable kind. It

[1] Similar to Unitarianism.

permeated the thinking of very many of the 'Moderate' ministers, and through their teaching, which was neutral when not negative, it influenced the lives of the people. It raised the standard of revolt against the authority of the Word of God, and in the name of common sense it vitiated not only the religion but the morals of those that gave place to it. The 'Moderate' ministers of Ayrshire, whose victim and tool Robert Burns came to be, were representatives of this school, and so strong was the movement away from the Reformed Faith that many of the leaders of the 'Moderates' sought the abolition of subscription to the Confession of Faith. It was this effort that led to the retirement in his later years of Principal Robertson from the leadership of the 'Moderate' party, as he did not approve of the wisdom of the course then taken by his fellows. This movement failed, but it was not the less significant and ominous for all that. John Love, however, was mercifully delivered from the snare, and while still a student he was soundly converted to God. The account of his spiritual exercises at the outset of his Christian course we have in the two volumes of Memorials which were published in 1857. And it is at least striking to remark the gentleness of his experience at his conversion when one considers how thorough and how searching the teaching of his later years was. These two memorial volumes give us his juvenile writings. They afford a specimen of a youthful giant. These are his first-fruits. In them we have the record of his searching self-scrutiny, and we learn how strong the influence of Jonathan Edwards and Thomas Shepard was on his inner life. Edwards and Brainerd were then the modern New Englanders, but Scotland had earlier and close ties with New England and American Puritanism. Rutherford, Durham, and Fraser of Brea reveal these. Wodrow from his manse of Eastwood was in correspondence with Cotton Mather. Witherspoon went

SOME FAVOURITE BOOKS

from Paisley to Princeton, and the intimacy of the pre-
vious century was kept up in the brotherly correspondence
of John Erskine, Gillespie, Gillies, and Maclaurin with
men like Prince and Edwards, and in the appointment of
David Brainerd as their missionary to the Indians by the
Scottish Society for Propagating Christian Knowledge. In
after years John Love edited, with notes, a Paisley edition
of Shepard's *Sincere Convert* and *Sound Believer*; and these
notes show how he had to weigh and sometimes to adjust
the balance of statements made by the worthy Puritan,
whose acquaintance he made in his formative years and
whose searching teaching had put him to the test.

THE MEMORIALS OF HIS EARLY PREACHING

At the age of twenty-seven John Love became assistant in
one of the churches of Greenock, a town where there was
a long and sound Evangelical tradition, and when there
he preached a series of sermons, or rather more than one
series, which appeared in print almost thirty years after
his death. These are a monument of the sustained power
of his early ministry, and they show the disciplined mind
and the chastened heart that he had from the very outset
of his public work. In his student days he waited on the
gospel preaching of his own neighbourhood alike in
Renfrew and in Ayrshire, and his teaching preserves and
reproduces the best strain of searching, scriptural evangelical preaching which worked so mightily among the
commonalty of Scotland. There were in the westland
Seceders and Cameronians[1] outside the Establishment
whose type of doctrine was of the same kind. They
helped to maintain the Reformed tradition, while the
presence and the working of unbelief, more or less

[1]Followers of Richard Cameron, the Covenanter. Strict Calvinists, they
regarded the 1688 Revolution Settlement as weak.

[40]

covert, among the 'Moderates' put the Evangelicals on their mettle and kept the edge of their weapons bright and keen.

THE PREACHING OF HIS LONDON YEARS

In August 1787 Dr Love was ordained to the ministry in one of the Scottish congregations in London – Crispin Street, Spitalfields. The sermon preached on that occasion by Mr Rutledge, and the charge delivered by Mr Smith, are in print. These London churches were, as a rule, held by men who stood for orthodox evangelism, and never had they a more worthy representative of their sentiments than in the young minister of Hoxton. In this charge, however, he was by no means so successful as he was after his return to Scotland. Preaching like his, so solid and majestic, so spiritual and searching, was rather much for the capacity or the taste of commercial Scotland in modern Babylon. Some of his sermons belonging to this period of his work have been published, and they show that if in the former century Robert Blair could so preach as to show the majesty of God, and in the intervening years Ebenezer Erskine could preach the Gospel in its majesty, this great majestic strain had not died out from the Scottish pulpit. In those London years the modern missionary movement took shape, and Love threw himself into it from the start. He was associated with Hill and Hardcastle and the other worthies who were the Fathers and Founders of the London Missionary Society, and whose lives are sketched by Dr John Morison in his memorial volume. In connection with this work he wrote his Otaheite Discourses to furnish a guide for applying divine truth to the minds of the unevangelised. These sermons are found in the miscellaneous volume of Dr Love's writings.

THE WRITINGS OF HIS RIPER YEARS

Early in the nineteenth century Dr Love was recalled to his native land to the Chapel of Ease at Anderston, which was then near Glasgow, though it is now almost in the heart of the city. Here a great congregation gathered about him, and he found his public. For the last twenty years of his life this charge was his field of labour, and he was the centre of a circle of like-minded worthies, the memory of whose brotherly intercourse was preserved by men like Nixon of Montrose, who knew them in his youthful days. Dr Balfour of the High Church was one of these – a man greatly beloved and a survivor of the earnest company of Lady Glenorchy's friends. Old Mr Oliphant of Dumbarton was another. In his Kilmarnock days he had the honour of coming under the lash of poor Burns. He was of Seceding upbringing, but joined the Establishment. He was of a somewhat earlier generation than Dr Love, on whom he leaned and whom he called 'Brotherly Love.' Then there was Kenneth Bayne of Greenock, Robertson of Rothesay, and Neil Macbride of Arran, with others of like spirit. With the three last named Dr Love took part in the great awakening of Arran, and the young men who from that island went forward to study for the gospel ministry came powerfully under his influence in their college days. There were such as Finlay Cook and his brother Archibald, and John Macalister, with others like them. They were the means of spreading and perpetuating his influence in the various fields in which they laboured. The monuments of this portion of his ministry are found, along with a number of his earlier discourses, in two volumes which appeared a few years after his death. Stewart of Cromarty had a godly aunt, Miss Stewart, who was matron of the Royal Infirmary, Glasgow. She was one of Dr Love's hearers, and through her, her nephew came into early touch with him and his set. The remark was once made to him that Love's published discourses were but skeletons. 'If that be so,' said Stewart, 'they are the bones of a mammoth.' There is one other volume one must have in order to get a full view of John Love. It is that of his letters, so much appreciated by a spiritual judge like Mary Winslow. They were edited by Peter Macbride of Rothesay, with a preface by Macdonald of Ferintosh. These are the relics of his pen, and they still have their own public. The folk that prized Dr Love were the folk that prized John Duncan, and they found ways and means to get 'the Rabbi' to Milton, Glasgow. And long may it be before Glasgow and the West of Scotland are without those to whom the memory of these men of God is fragrant!

7: John Willison on *The Sabbath*

Our old writers furnish the Church in Scotland with a wealth of sound theology, and among the literature of religious homes few books found a warmer place among our forebears than those of John Willison of Dundee.

AN AGE OF CONTROVERSY

Willison was the contemporary of Boston and the Erskines' and in the shire of Forfar he had just such work to do in his day as they had further south. When the Synod was much more a living court in our churches than it has come to be, he had a special field of work and post of influence in the Synod of Angus and Mearns. As yet the old feudal jurisdiction was not a thing of the past and in his neighbourhood the family influence of the Ogilvies and the Carnegies was cast on the side of the Stuarts. The building up of the Reformed and restored Church of the Revolution Settlement[1] was uphill work. Dundee itself was a stronghold of Jacobite sentiment, and extant pamphlets still record the bitter conflict between the inert Episcopacy of the 'College' faction and the aggressively militant bigotry of the 'Usagers' in the Episcopal community of the town. Where the Romanising leaven of

[1]It followed on the enthronement of William III and Mary II after the Revolution of 1688, Anglican clergy who refused to take the oath of allegiance to the new monarchs were called Non-Jurors. Some among the last-named who clung to high-church practices were termed usagers.

Nonjuring divinity was at work, one might take it for granted that Presbyterians, who were such indeed, would be put upon their mettle. This was the case. And irenical and brotherly as the spirit of John Willison was, he was called into controversy in defence of the Reformed Church against the polemics of the Jacobites.

CONTENDING FOR THE FAITH

But to make things livelier still, Willison had a neighbour who was not a Jacobite, and from whom he met with no small trouble. This was John Glas of Tealing, who, for years before he left his charge in the Church of Scotland, was following courses that led to Independency. When at last he took a separate position, Glas became the founder of the old Scots Independents – sometimes called the Glassites, after their founder, and sometimes the Sandemanians, after his son-in-law, David Sandeman, who became the leading exponent of the type of teaching and Church life for which the body stood. Willison, as the defender of the faith, was called upon to engage in controversy with Glas, and he maintained the middle ground of the Reformed Church as against the right-hand extremes of Glas, and the left-hand defections of unevangelical Episcopacy. It is interesting to note that the movement originated at Tealing was the head-waters of Scottish Voluntaryism.[1]

In this matter of standing for his Church, however, Willison had still another battle to fight. Moderatism had begun to lift up its unbelieving head. Its organised subservience to an earthly allegiance was going hand in hand with a despotic policy towards the Christian people

[1] The view (generally disapproved by the Scottish Reformed Churches) that 'the State, as the State, has nothing to do with religion'.

of the land. This brought about the Secession, and the type of men and teaching that Willison represented felt the shock. Along with like-minded brethren he bestirred himself to heal the breach. But their efforts were futile. They, however, went to show how strong the Evangelical element in the Church still was, and what it might have managed to do in the way of keeping things on right lines, had its representatives only been as wide awake and as well-organised as those men were who had got the reins in their hands.

Even after Willison's days Witherspoon could beat Robertson in the General Assembly. But he could do so only by using his adversary's weapons. He had to drill his supporters and to keep them in hand. When he did so, he could show to what an extent, even in the middle of the eighteenth century, the ministry of the Church of Scotland adhered to her historic principles. The weakness of the orthodox was that they did not organise with sufficient care, or if by fits and starts they did so, they did not keep up the organisation that their more astute and politic opponents maintained.

HIS WRITINGS

In connection with his efforts to keep the Church on safe lines, Willison not only succeeded in carrying the Assembly with him in action designed to bring back the Seceders; he is credited with having a great hand in passing the admirable Act of the General Assembly in 1736 on Gospel preaching. The Evangel was coming to be conspicuous by its absence from the preaching of the Moderates, and Assembly action was taken to impress on the Ministry a sense of their duty as heralds of the Cross. It would be well, if our Churches had been alive to the working of such tendencies as culminated in the apostasy of the later eighteenth century. For the revolution of the wheel of history has brought Scotland round to a midnight darkness of which the deepest depth of Moderatism was but a shadow. The other piece of work that he did in this connection was the drawing up of his *Testimony on behalf of the present Truth*. This is a mild and temperate document that reflects the gentlemanly spirit of the writer and gives a pleasing impression of how firmly, and yet how courteously he could stand in defence of the cause of God.

But one will find that the bulk of Willison's writings consists of his practical works. Among these his *Sacramental Meditations*, and his *Afflicted Man's Companion* are well known. But more extensive than these are his Catechetic exercises. He was an indefatigable catechist, and Scottish folk will not forget his little *Mother's Catechism*. Nor should we omit the fact that his *Exposition of the Shorter Catechism* was translated into Gaelic, and played its part in the instruction of our Highland counties during the great Evangelical movement of a century ago.

But we have spent our time and space in speaking of works other than that on the sanctification of the Sabbath. Along with Daniel Wilson's (of Calcutta) seven sermons on the Lord's Day, this work is mentioned by no mean judge as the best on the subject in the English language. Such was the estimate of the godly Bishop Ryle of Liverpool, and we, the countrymen of Willison, should not let it out of sight as out of mind. It is found in the collected writings of the author of which there are three editions at least, and by itself in a most convenient form, it was one of Taylor's Edinburgh Large Type Cabinet Library. Those that have not got it should look it out, and those that have, should read it.

8: John Blackader's *Memoirs*

'The first three' of the field preachers, as they were called in Galloway in the times of persecution, were John Welsh of Irongray, Gabriel Semple of Carsphairn, and John Blackader of Troqueer. They were all men of the highest standing among the suffering Presbyterians. If only the materials were available for writing it, the life of John Welsh, the heroic great-grandson of John Knox, would read like a sensational romance. Semple lived to see the Presbyterian Church restored at the Glorious Revolution of 1688, but both his comrades had passed away before their church came out of her furnace experience. Fortunately, we have an extended account of the life and varied adventures of John Blackader, and there are few books that cast more light on the state of his times than his *Memoirs*, edited in 1823 by Andrew Crichton. This work is based mainly on two manuscripts, one written by Blackader himself when a prisoner on the Bass Rock, and the other an account of his sufferings, written by his son. The book appeared at a time when the researches of Dr M'Crie began to bear fruit, and an interest was taken in the witness and sufferings of the Covenanters, which helped largely to prepare the mind of Scotland for the revival of their principles that culminated in the Disruption of 1843. The editor's work links together the information furnished by his authorities, and as these are chiefly first hand in their character the reader is brought into close touch with the actors in the scenes that are described.

HIS EARLY LIFE

John Blackader was the head of an ancient family which, however, by his time, had fallen into decay. They belonged to the Merse,[1] but for a number of generations before his time their chief seat was at Tulliallan. He was born in 1615 and studied at Glasgow University, when his mother's brother was Principal. In the year 1653 he was settled at Troqueer, near Dumfries, and there he remained until 1662 when with more than three hundred of his brethren he was excluded from his charge by the policy of the Drunken Parliament. He was not prepared to comply with the Episcopacy which Charles and Sharp forced on the Church established in Scotland. Nor could he acknowledge the royal supremacy in church affairs for which the new regime stood.

HIS EJECTION FROM TROQUEER

When the last Sabbath of October 1662 arrived, it was the closing day of Blackader's ministry in his charge. His sermon that day was interrupted by the coming of the military, who, it was found, came to apprehend him. Many of the people went away but some followed their minister to the manse, where he finished the sermon that had been cut short. But when he was done his hearers lingered as though they were unwilling to go away. He asked them to give no handle to their adversaries but to disperse peaceably. 'Go,' he said, 'and fend for yourselves: the hour is come when the shepherd is smitten and the flock shall be scattered. Many are this day mourning the desolations of Israel and weeping like the prophet between the porch and the altar. God's heritage has

[1]Berwickshire.

become the prey of the spoiler: the mountain of the Lord's house as the high places of the forest. When the faithful pastors are removed hirelings shall intrude, whom the Great Shepherd never sent, who will devour the flock and tread down the residue with their feet. As for me I have done my duty and now there is no time to evade. I recommend you to Him who is able to keep you from falling, and am ready through grace to be disposed of as the Lord pleases.' Before the week had run out he left the parish and found refuge with his cousin, the wife of Ferguson of Caitloch, in Glencairn, a family that suffered much in these trying days. He had scarcely left his home when it was raided by rough soldiers sent to seize him. One of his sons tells the story of the search after him and its failure, and of the eviction that then took place. 'Immediately after we were forced to pack up bag and baggage and to remove to Glencairn, ten miles from Troqueer. We, who were children, were put into cadger's creels,[1] where one of us cried out coming through the Bridgend of Dumfries, "I'm banished, I'm banished." One happened to ask, "Who has banished you, my bairn?" He answered, "Bite-the-sheep has banished me"'. Thus were the Blackaders driven from Troqueer.

A FIELD PREACHER

Within a few months after his extrusion from his charge he began, along with his two neighbours, Welsh and Semple, his adventurous work as a field-preacher. In this he did not spare himself, and some of the most interesting accounts we have of the conventicles held by the *outed* ministers are from his pen. He was at the great gathering at the Hill of Beath in Fife, preached at Bo'ness and

[1] Hawkers' baskets.

Lilliesleaf, and officiated at the great communions at Irongray and East Nisbet. The narrative he gives of the scene at East Nisbet is worthy of all the praise that has often been given it, and will bear to be reproduced. In the midst of his unceasing labours he regretted that he did not have the tongue of the wild Highlanders that he might preach to them the Christ he preached so freely to others. The expansive Evangelical zeal that he showed in this found utterance in words that he often used that he would be content to go a thousand miles on foot to have had the Highland tongue. His zeal was tempered with caution and in the midst of his eventful wanderings he did not lose the culture which one of his education and upbringing might be expected to possess. It came out in his popular preaching, which the godly who were learned admired, while the godly who were unlearned and simple heard with profit and delight.

INTERNAL DISSENSIONS

In the heat of the furnace of the Killing times[1] the witnesses were sundered, and some of whom better might have been expected accepted the Royal Indulgence, and so far seemed to connive at the Supremacy which they professed to reject. Other brethren took an extreme course of separating from those who took the Indulgence and from all who would not separate along with them. Blackader used his best endeavours, while keeping free from both extremes, to keep the suffering kirk from being broken into fragments. This exposed him, in spite of his own unmistakable witness, to misconstruction on the part of Cameron's followers. And there is one sad instance of

---

[1]*Fair Sunshine* by Jock Purves supplies a fairly detailed account of these 'times'. It is still in print (Banner of Truth).

the refusal of some of them in Annandale to welcome his ministry because he would not go the full length they went in separating from the Indulged, though he was hunted for his faithfulness like a partridge on the mountains. Oppression maketh a wise man mad. To allay the dissensions among the persecuted Presbyterians Blackader sailed to Holland and succeeded in bringing the exiles in Rotterdam to be more of one mind than they were. The quarrel between Macward and Fleming was so far healed. But with these dissensions a new leaven began to work among the persecuted in regard to the unity of the Church, and the persecution that could not crush, succeeded in sundering, the witnesses for Christ's Crown and Covenant.

THE BASS ROCK

Not long after his return to Scotland Blackader was taken and sent as a prisoner to the Bass Rock, where he spent the last five years of his life. Dying early in 1686 he was buried at North Berwick, and his gravestone bears an epitaph in verse superior to most of those carved in rude letters on the stones of the martyrs and one that gives vigorous expression to the virtues of the redoubtable worthy whom it commemorates.

Blest John, for Jesus' sake, in Patmos bound,
His prison Bethel, Patmos Pisgah found;
So the bless'd John, on yonder rock confined,
His body suffered but no chains could bind
His heaven-aspiring soul; while day by day,
As from Mount Pisgah's top he did survey
The promised land, and viewed the crown by faith
Laid up for those who faithful are till death.
Grace formed him in the Christian Hero's mould
Meek in his own concerns, in's Master's bold;

Passions to Reason chained, Prudence did lead
Zeal warmed his breast and Reason cooled his head.
Five years on the lone rock, yet sweet abode,
He Enoch-like enjoyed and walked with God;
Till, by long living on this heavenly food,
His soul by love grew up too great, too good
To be confined to jail as flesh and blood.
Death broke his fetters off, then swift he fled
From sin and sorrow; and, by angels led
Entered the mansions of eternal joy;
Blest soul, thy warfare's done, praise, love, enjoy.
His dust here rests till Jesus come again
Even so, blest Jesus, come – come, Lord – Amen.

9: Thomas M'Crie's *Life of John Knox*

It is now more than a hundred years since Thomas M'Crie published the work with which his name has been ever since associated, the work that made his name known, and gave him a foremost place among the writers of history, and the work that was itself a critically successful battle fought for the good cause for which the writer stood.

THE REFORMERS UNDER A CLOUD

The name and fame of our Reformers, Confessors, and Martyrs had come to be overspread with a cloud of obloquy and misunderstanding. The Union[1] which made England the predominant partner in a United Great Britain brought the educated classes under influences which, so far as they were religious or ecclesiastical, were strongly Anglican. And Anglicanism from the time that it passed under the eclipsing shadow of the school of Laud was not distinguished for its love to the Reformers or its zeal for their teaching. The influence of Clarendon and regnant Episcopacy told on the judgment of literary men, and the decay of spiritual religion in the reaction of the eighteenth century taught an unbelieving generation to look down on those men of God to whom Britain owed her Reformation. Such historians as Hume and Robertson could not be expected to do much to correct mistaken

[1] Act of union (1707). Henceforward Great Britain had one Parliament.

impressions here, for they were almost equally out of sympathy with the faith and life of the worthies who broke the keys of Rome.

In Scotland, Moderatism meant spiritual indifference which will never give a warm place in its cold heart to the life and zeal that godliness demands and illustrates. Men of this tendency could pass in a frigid fashion a favourable judgment on the struggles of the sixteenth and seventeenth centuries as the birth throes of modern freedom. But they felt themselves in a more congenial atmosphere when they consorted with Royalists and reactionaries than when they read the records of sturdy Reformers, and Puritans, and Covenanters. In the Church of Scotland, there were representatives of another strain, but too many even of these had felt the spirit of the age, and learned to apologise in a shamefaced kind of way for what were called the heats and the excesses of their ancestors.

SECESSION DECLENSION

Among the Seceders of various classes there was a truer estimate of what the world owed to the leaders of the Reformation, and the covenanting struggle. But by the end of the eighteenth century the zeal of the early Seccession had begun to die away. A generation arose that were more interested in the present, with its political problems, than in the past with its principles and traditions. Seceders came to look on themselves as rival Churches to the Church of Scotland, and not as a Secession from it, and so on a large scale there was a falling away from the profession of their fathers. While still a young man, M'Crie was called to make a stand against this tendency. This laid him under the necessity of making a thorough search into the origins, principles, and early contendings of the Protestant Reformation, and of the Church which adhered loyally to it. When the branch of the Secession to which he belonged, tampered with their testimony he with a few of his seniors in the ministry refused to compromise themselves by forsaking the principles for which they had hitherto stood.

THE 'STATEMENT OF DIFFERENCES'

In defence of his action, and that of his brethren he issued his first important work. This was his 'Statement of Differences' which set forth the significance and far-reaching character of the changes adopted by the General Associate Synod in their revised Testimony. Bruce of Whitburn, his theological tutor, Aitken of Kirriemuir, and Chalmers of Haddington, were his associates who lived to keep up the fight, and they were all men of mark. But the youngest of the four had laid upon him the task of expounding the differences between the Old and the New Testimony, and thus the honour was his of giving the first, and perhaps the ablest exposure of the real genius of the voluntaryism that had sapped the steadfastness of profession alike among the Burghers, and the Antiburghers. The very being of the Secession,[1] if it was to be kept on its early lines, demanded on the part of its advocates and defenders a careful study of the history of that Church from the prevailing party in whose judicatories they declared and maintained a Secession. The call to study these things never met with a more worthy response than that yielded to it by the biographer of John Knox.

[1]The Secession in the Presbyterian Church in the mid-1730s which produced the Seceders was 'broken in two' in 1747 by a dispute as to whether or not Seceders could consistently swear a certain clause in the oath taken by the free burgesses of a few Scottish towns. The two parties became known as the Burghers and the Anti-burghers. Some years later further differences separated Old Lights from New Lights.

THE LIFE OF KNOX

M'Crie held that those of his name ripened late in life, and never did much before they were forty. He was almost that age when his chief work appeared. When it was announced, influential Church dignitaries of evangelical and Whig proclivities, like Sir Henry Moncrieff, Wellwood, looked for little from an Old Light Antiburgher Seceder. They might expect perhaps an expansion of honest John Howie,[1] or, at the best, a book rooted in the past though noble in its tone, like Wilson of Perth's *Defence of Reformation Principles*.[2] But never were men more taken aback when the reality shamed their anticipations. The literary world discovered that in historical studies a star of the first magnitude swam into their ken, and that a defender of our old worthies had arisen who was able to meet the whole tribe of detractors and nibblers, and that he was a man of masculine intellect, and of disciplined powers who must be reckoned with as one of the most powerful forces in the religious life of his generation.

What first brought the work into the prominence that it merited was the Review that Professor Dugald Stewart wrote of it in the then young *Edinburgh Review*. Stewart was then at the height of his reputation. His attention was drawn to the work in a singular manner. His man-servant was one of M'Crie's congregation, and he got his minister's book when it was published. Soon after, his master rang time and again for him, but got no answer. He went to see what was up, and found his man deep in a book – so deeply absorbed indeed as not to have noticed the bell that had summoned him. The Professor's curiosity was awakened as to the book that had so captivated his

[1] Author of *Scots Worthies* (1774).
[2] William Wilson (1690-1741), born in Glasgow, ministered in Perth after 1716, and produced his *Defence of the Reformation Principles of the Church of Scotland* in 1739.

servant. He got it and read it for himself, saw its strength, assessed it at its high value, and let the world know what a treasure it was. It soon sold, and the vogue it met with was the turning of the tide in regard to the understanding and appreciation of the principles of the Reformed Church in Scotland. Before the revival of these principles came to a head, the Ten Years' Conflict was fought, and the Disruption (1843) rent the Church in twain. This it did because our rulers refused to the awakened Church the constitutional rights for which her fathers had fought and bled. And those who remained in the State Church did so at the expense of sacrificing the Church's spiritual freedom and the crown rights of her Head.

Thus was this book a critical victory for the principles of its hero. The attention it drew to them was only deepened by the writer's next work, his *Life of Melville*. This deals with the fight with Erastianism. Royal interference with the Church was the taproot of the difficulties in which she was involved until at the Revolution she was established in her dearly won freedom. But time and space fail us in drawing attention to this fireside treasure. We may find another opportunity of dealing with the writings of the great Thomas M'Crie.

10: John Colquhoun on *The Covenant of Grace*

In the life of Dr Moody Stuart the story is told of how he and his brother when they were students together in Edinburgh in the early nineteenth century, made up their minds to walk to their home in Paisley at the close of the Session. They set off towards the end of the week and spent from Saturday to Monday at a wayside inn. On the evening of Saturday they observed the arrival of two respectable young working men, who spent the night in the inn. Having left early on Sabbath morning they came back again in the evening. The students found out who they were and what their errand was. They were seriously exercised Christian lads who were working near Glasgow. They had heard a preacher to their mind and determined to wait on his ministry as often as they could. The preacher was the then venerable Dr Colquhoun of the New Kirk in South Leith, and in order to hear him the young men set off after their work was done on Saturday, spent the night at the halfway inn, set off early on Sabbath morning, reached Leith and heard the aged Doctor twice, then returned to their inn to spend the night. They were to rise early on Monday that they might reach their work in good time in the morning. Thus they walked not much less than a hundred miles each week to hear the preaching of the Word. It must have been no common preaching that drew them so far and it must have been no common eagerness to wait upon the Word that prompted them.

They were but specimens of the many in Scotland that set the highest value on the preaching of the great 'Marrow' Divine.

Dr Colquhoun[1] was the contemporary of Dr John Love, whom he outlived a few years, and whose senior he was. They entered Glasgow University about the same time, and from the start of their public life they were outspoken heralds of the Cross. At the close of one of his first sermons John Colquhoun was addressed as he came down from the pulpit by an aged woman who had been a hearer. 'That's you,' said she. 'Go, spend and be spent for Him.' 'Oh ay,' was his answer, 'but no a' in ae day.' Zeal warmed his breast but reason cooled his head. In days when the blight of a deadly unbelieving Moderatism lay on much of the Church of Scotland, Love and he were pillars of strength on the side of a firm and powerful gospel. Their names were known by the godly throughout the land, and in the homely speech of a North Country worthy who prized them highly, when they and their contemporary Mr Robertson of Kingussie were taken away within three years, 'they were the hoops that kept the staves of the old cask together.' So much of the old Whig Revolution order passed with them, for they were hardly gone when Rome won her way into the British legislature. Like their contemporary M'Crie, these men saw how dangerous the outcome of this encroachment was likely to be.

AN ARDENT EVANGELICAL

The 'Marrow' theology found its chief home in the eighteenth century in the various branches of the Seces-

[1] John Colquhoun (1748–1827) born at Luss in Dumbartonshire, was a shepherd and a weaver before he entered Glasgow university. In 1781 he became minister in South Leith and remained in South Leith until his death 46 years later.

sion; but it was not without its able exponents in the Church Established, and of these none was better known or more highly regarded than John Colquhoun. For the first quarter of the following century he and John Brown of Whitburn were perhaps the most outstanding representatives of this school. The latter wrote his *Life of Hervey* and his *Gospel Truth Accurately Stated* to exhibit the old theology of his fathers. The former began his career as author in his mature years, and his different works embody and enshrine the teaching of a lifetime. The fullest of them is his view of the Covenant of Grace. Its strain of doctrine is not essentially different from that of quite a number of others. He wrote on Spiritual Comfort, on Saving Faith, on Evangelical Repentance, on the Covenant of Works, on Law and Gospel, on the Promises, and a valuable Sacramental Catechism. After his death a small volume of his sermons appeared with a sketch of his life.

In his riper years he and Dr Davidson of the Tolbooth Kirk, Edinburgh, were the patriarchs of old Evangelicalism in and near the metropolis. Dr Davidson became Davidson of Muirhouse, though by birth he was a Randall, and the name Randall which was his in early life found in him the second of his family that bore signal witness on behalf of the Evangel in the days of the Moderate ascendancy. In the early part of the nineteenth century serious-minded aspirants to the ministerial office sought the company and the counsel of these fathers. In this connection a tradition survives which shows how in his own way Dr Colquhoun reconciled his respect for findings of the General Assembly with his uncompromising maintenance of the teaching of Boston and his fellows. Students would ask him what books they should read and he gave them advice. 'Noo, ye ken, I daurna advise ye to read the "Marrow", for the Assembly condemned it; but

though they condemned the "Marrow" they didna con-
demn Tammas Bcwston's notes on the "Marrow", and
that's a book that ye should read.' Our old worthies
attached great weight to the Acts of the General Assembly
even when they did not altogether approve of them. In his
own early days, after he was brought to the knowledge of
the truth through the labours of an agent of the S.P.C.K.,
John Colquhoun had walked all the way from Luss to
Glasgow to buy a copy of Boston's *Fourfold State*, and the
influence that told on his first days he wished to bring to
bear on the rising ministry.

HIS CONTEMPORARIES

Dr Macdonald of Ferintosh, during the years of his work
in the Gaelic Church of Edinburgh, enjoyed intimate
acquaintance with Dr Colquhoun. David Black of Lady
Yester's had been taken away while yet young, but there
was a goodly brotherhood in the ministry then in Edinburgh and Leith. Walter Buchanan was in the Canongate,
and Colquhoun's friend and neighbour, the friend of the
blind and the founder of the Blind Asylum in Edinburgh,
Dr Johnston of North Leith, was another. Another, to
name no more, was Dr Jones of Lady Glenorchy's. This
Calvinistic Methodist and the old Marrowman, whose
funeral service he lived to preach, were knit together.
Though a Welshman and accustomed to the laxer
psalmody that prevailed in the great Methodist movement
to the south of the Tweed, Thomas Jones came to be so
satisfied with the exclusive use of the Psalter as the
Church's hymnbook that he put the Paraphrases which
were bound up with it out of action. In this he was at one
with Colquhoun. The one had the Paraphrases sewn up,
the other had them cut out. Perhaps the last survivor in
public life that perpetuated the good traditions of the

chapel in South Leith was that magnificent specimen of the Old School Free Churchman, Rev. A. M. Bannatyne, whose youth was nurtured under the pastorate of Dr Colquhoun.

TWO NOTED CATECHISTS

Not only did Macdonald of Ferintosh and his fellows in the Northern Evangelical ministry make the name of Dr Colquhoun known in the North and North-West of Scotland, there were two noted catechists who bore the stamp of his teaching. John Macdonald of Urquhart, who was S.P.C.K. teacher at Bunloit on Loch Ness side, was one of these. Of him Dr Kennedy of Dingwall speaks as the Turretin of the 'men' who used to gather to Redcastle in his father's days. He was a masterly, systematic Divine. The other was Donald Mackenzie, the warm and loving friend of Kennedy of Redcastle, who stood by him in all his trials in Assynt. Donald had a good and godly education at the feet of his uncle Hector, an old soldier, who in his turn had been trained by his uncle, Roderick Mackenzie, who preached for some time at Nigg, the outpost of the Secession in the North, and assisted at the settlement of the second Thomas Boston when he left the Church of Scotland and his father's parish of Ettrick to be settled over the Relief congregation in Jedburgh. Donald was in the Reay Fencibles on garrison duty in Leith when, to use his own words, under the preaching of Dr Colquhoun, life was put in the form of godliness that he had as the fruit of his uncle's teaching. A number of the fruits of John Kennedy's preaching in Assynt became teachers under the Gaelic Schools Society. They were the younger comrades of Donald Mackenzie, and in this as in other ways the name and work of Dr Colquhoun came to be widely known in the Gaelic Highlands in the halcyon days of the Evangelical Revival. No mean share in that work was borne by the Gaelic School teachers. But apart from this way of spreading his name among his fellow Highlanders, the evangelical Mr Nairn of Dunsinane was at the cost of securing a translation into Gaelic of part of Colquhoun on the *Covenant of Grace*, and thus his teaching played a part in moulding the Highlands and Islands in the generation that made the Disruption the thorough thing that it was in the North and North-West of Scotland. Occasionally, but seldom, a copy of this translation is to be met with.

Those that know and prize the writings of John Colquhoun are not as many as they once were, but anyone that wishes to acquaint himself with one of the best specimens of the sane, evangelical and experimental divinity that our fathers loved could not be better guided than to look out and read the savoury treatise we have taken as the tenth of our Favourite Books.[1]

[1] In 1965 Banner of Truth reprinted Dr Colquhoun's treatise *Repentance* (paperback 159 pp.) first published in 1826.

11: *The Life of the Haldanes*

In the last year of the eighteenth century there was a shaking among the dry bones. The fermentation that worked itself out in Revolutionary excesses in France might have powerfully influenced this country and changed the course of its history, had it not been for the working of the Evangelical Revival. In the Church of Scotland, Moderatism had for years held the reins of power, and over large districts of the land there was scarcely the glimmer of gospel witness except among the Seceders. Even among them a type of preaching began to manifest itself which failed to discriminate among their hearers and laid less stress than was due upon the need for the new birth. Though as a body they were leaving their old ground, they still maintained a witness for the doctrines of the Cross. There were many evangelicals in the ministry of the Church of Scotland, and in some parts of the land these were at the meridian of their influence. But taking Scotland as a whole one might well say that it was drifting away from the warm Evangelicalism of the sixteenth and seventeenth centuries. As the voice of the Evangel was silenced the restraints of godliness and of the good order that the Reformed Church stood for were removed. A negative and lifeless pulpit spread a fatal blight, and godlessness unrestrained and unblushing walked in the light of day. Economic changes were on foot and Revolution after the pattern of America and France might well have tried conclusions with the ancient constitution but for the revival of serious religion that set in. This revival strengthened the hands of constituted authority and an evangelised population learned to honour the king as they feared God. Christian principle taught them to bear with the ills of their lot and to look higher than the fleeting good of earth. The shortsighted leaders of political reaction and the purblind leaders of a sleeping Church failed to discern the character of the Evangelical movement and confused its activities with those of Revolution. Its missionary zeal made it suspect, as though it were the working of an evil thing that sought to turn the world upside down. No doubt in a way it was seeking to do this, but it was seeking to do it by setting a topsy-turvy world right by infusing into its spirit the fear of God. Among the representatives of this movement no more striking figures are seen than the two godly brothers, Robert and James Alexander Haldane.

THEIR EARLY LIFE

The Haldanes were the representatives of one of the old families of the Scottish aristocracy. Robert, the older of the two, was proprietor of the fine estate of Airthray, near Stirling, and James held the lucrative post of Captain of an East India-man. In his youth Robert too served at sea. Their near relative Admiral Duncan was the victor at Camperdown (1797), and early in the twentieth century the ancestral estate of the Haldanes at Gleneagles reverted to a scion of James's stock on the death of the late Lord Camperdown. When they were still young men both the brothers came under the power of the gospel, and at the outset of their Christian life they were in close touch with the living evangelical circles about Dr John Erskine of Greyfriars, Edinburgh, and John Newton of London. It was the age of Missionary and Tract Societies. The hearts of

Christians were opened to seek the spread of the gospel at home and abroad, and Robert Haldane sold his property with a view to the establishment of a mission in India. The heathenish policy of the East India Company whose Directorate were not yet under the spell of Charles Grant put a veto on the scheme.[1] But before the eighteenth century passed away the younger brother had begun his evangelical career in the Home Field. His early efforts were in the villages around Edinburgh. Then along with like-minded companions he went on extended tours in the North and West of Scotland. They reached Shetland in their work, and in Caithness and other parts which had their own share of Moderatism, Captain Haldane's preaching was rightly blessed. The account given of those tours in the *Life* is an interesting document, but in some details it is inaccurate. In the Gaelic belt through which the preachers passed, their ignorance of the language of the people limited their usefulness and shut them out from an appreciation of the amount of lively religion that was then to be found in the Northern Highlands. In the *Life of Campbell of Kingsland*, who was one of James Haldane's companions, there are interesting glimpses of their intercourse with some of the 'men' in the Inverness district. It was in connection with the countenance that he gave to the irregular preaching of Captain Haldane that the godly George Cowie of Huntly was driven out of the Antiburgher body. This was the occasion of the spread of

---

[1]Charles Grant was born in Inverness-shire on the 16th April, 1746, the day when Bonnie Prince Charlie was put to flight at the Battle of Culloden. His father was killed at the battle a few hours after his son's birth, fighting for the Prince. At the age of 21, Grant obtained a post with the East India Company. During a voyage to India in 1772 he began a lifelong friendship with the famous Danish missionary Christian Frederick Schwartz. Later he met with much success in countering the East India Company's enmity to Christian work in India. He introduced Sunday Schools into Scotland. An Episcopalian, he belonged to the Clapham Sect. He died in 1823.

missionary churches along the south seaboard of the Moray Firth and in Aberdeenshire.

JAMES HALDANE'S MINISTRY

This evangelism in its aggressive operations in the field of home heathenism came to be known as the Tabernacle Movement. From a felt necessity of the situation it became Independent, and the existence of the Independent or Congregational Churches in Scotland dates mainly from this epoch. For many years alike before and after the movement split over the question of baptism, it was soundly evangelical, though in later years its complexion changed considerably. For James Haldane there was built a large Tabernacle in Edinburgh, and after his early tours he settled down to be the pastor of the congregation that was built up there, and his brother, whose voice did not fit him for such public work as James undertook, became his righthand man. In this Tabernacle, which still stands in Leith Walk, good work was done among high and low.[1] Andrew Thomson found in his West End parish of St George's that many of his communicants traced the beginning of their spiritual life to the impressions of truth they had got in the Tabernacle. Thomas M'Crie (and what saner judge could one have?) pronounced the eulogy on James Haldane's preaching that he set forth the doctrine of Justification by Faith as purely and powerfully as any man of his day. In their later years, when Wardlaw and some of his followers went off the line as to the extent of the Atonement, James Haldane was not behindhand with his defence of an effectual Atonement. In his earlier years, and until some time after he had become a Baptist, he had marked crotchets in his ideas as to Church and Worship,

[1] At the present time (1988) a cinema occupies the Tabernacle's former sight.

but along with Robert he matured and mellowed and avoided extravagances as successfully as most of the worthies of his day. His aristocratic connections brought him in contact with the upper classes in both Scotland and England, and among them he was the means of doing much good.

ROBERT HALDANE'S WORK

Robert was the generous supporter of the Missionary and Biblical Societies, and in this connection he became the leader in the crusade for the spread of a pure Bible. As a Director of the British and Foreign Bible Society he found that on the Continent it pursued a policy of compromise and circulated the Apocrypha along with the Bible. This was in contravention of its own constitution. He fought the question out, and to him more than to any man is it due that an uncorrupted Bible is the heritage of the English-speaking world, for the bitter Apocrypha controversy, which split the Bible Society, secured to all intents and purposes that the Apocrypha was ousted from our English Bible. And the parent Society that refused to accept his honest guidance in its Foreign policy was constrained to conform to its constitution more closely than some of its leading spirits were disposed to do. In connection with this matter we may detect the first entrance of a Rationalistic leaven into the Evangelical Churches of Britain. It was introduced by his opponents, and very markedly by pronounced voluntaries among them, who tried to white-wash the Directors of the Bible Society. Haldane's chief support was Dr Andrew Thomson in the *Edinburgh Christian Instructor*. And the men of God who became the Disruption Fathers were almost without exception on the same side. Co-operation in these matters brought Robert Haldane into intimate fellowship with Dr Robert Gordon in particular, so that in his last days – he died in 1842 – his dearest friends, apart from his brother James, were found among the men that led the Evangelical party in the Church of Scotland. Though he espoused Baptist views at the same time as his brother, his zeal for these cooled to such an extent that in his long intercourse with French-speaking Protestants he was taken to be a Scottish Presbyterian.

The mention of the French-speaking churches calls up to mind his wonderful work among them both at Geneva and at Montauban. After Waterloo gave peace to Europe, Robert Haldane spent a winter in Geneva. There he came to know the students of divinity, and found that in the city of Calvin and Turretin heathen Socinianism was rampant. He held for the young men classes in his hotel, and most of the two dozen or so that attended became sound and hearty evangelists. Malan and Gaussen and D'Aubigné and the Monods, Adolphe and Frederic, represent the best strain of Continental Protestantism in the nineteenth century, and their work was the outcome of the moment-ous winter that Robert Haldane spent at Geneva. The *Life* which records the work of the two brothers is from the pen of James's son, Alexander, who, as editor of the *Record*, was along with the godly Earl of Shaftesbury for the years of his public life, the lay leader of thought among English Church Evangelicals. One would expect in such a case that it would be written in full sympathy with the Evangelical work of his worthy father and uncle. So it is, and a heartening book it is for those that are interested in the great movements of the gospel in the Church of God.

12: J. C. Ryle's *Christian Leaders of the 18th Century*

The Evangelical Revival of the eighteenth century found godliness at a low level in England. But it wrought a wonderful change. The end of the seventeenth century showed that Protestant sentiment had still a great hold on the Church of England, though more than a quarter of a century had passed since the expulsion of the unyielding Puritans. But the upheaval that brought about the Revolution was not followed in any marked degree with a revival of religion in the southern kingdom. In this respect there was a striking difference between Scotland and England.

By the beginning of the eighteenth century the last of the Puritan witnesses were passing fast away, and few of those who rose to fill their places were worthy of them. Those in the Established Church that might still be called doctrinal Puritans were few and far between. A kind of teaching that was neither law nor gospel was supplanting the sound speech that could not be condemned which characterised so much of the seventeenth-century pulpit. A vanishing gospel was symptomatic of decay in godliness. With the spread of fashionable Deism in the higher classes, and of an unevangelical strain of preaching among the Nonconformists, the flame of witness borne to the Evangel for wellnigh two hundred years was flickering as though it were about to go out. The light of the candle, which a burning Latimer and Ridley lit, was not what it had been. But among the embers that smouldered on the altar the fire was still alive, and it could be fanned into a flame. Yet it burned low.

The Dissenters kicked against subscription to doctrinal articles that pledged them to profess the mysteries of the faith. They looked upon it as a yoke of bondage. From tolerating Arian denials of the mystery of godliness, they passed on, to a large extent, to an Arianism that left them no atoning sacrifice and no divine Saviour. Before the century was out, those that followed this line of things reached, in the advance of their apostasy, the depths of Socinianism. The tolerance of Arian fellowship told in the first quarter of the century how much the zeal of the Dissenting interest for the witness and ways of their fathers had cooled. It was a token of the waning of the day of gospel power. And when the evangelical message became a stranger in the pulpits, the fruits of its working came to be strangers in the lives of the people.

The withering breath that wrought such havoc among the Presbyterian congregations of England – and most of the ejected Puritans were Presbyterians – brought a like blight upon the Church of England. When Joseph Butler, in 1736, published his *Analogy*, he could speak of how the impression had come to prevail in wide circles that it was now understood that the gospel was an imposture, a man-exploded fable. But for isolated witnesses here and there throughout the land, the preaching of the doctrines of grace was a thing of the past, and in this respect the second quarter of the eighteenth century was not unlike the first quarter of the twentieth.

A NEW-BORN EVANGELISM

But the darkest hour went before the dawn. The light that burned low was to blaze up again, and men of God were raised up to do noble work for their Lord and His cause. The book of which we write is a record of their life and doings. The outcome of their work appeared in the leavening of England with a new-born evangelism. The Dissenting interest, which had long been languishing, showed signs of restored vitality, and many of the older Independent and Baptist Churches date from the middle of the eighteenth century. Lady Huntingdon did her part, and it was no small one. And Wesleyan societies sprang up all over the land. But, apart from the effects of the movement that thus manifested themselves outside the establishment, there arose a school of preachers within its pale whose labours changed the face of the Church of England, and before a hundred years had run from the outset of the Revival, the Evangelical party could almost claim that it had secured the leadership of the Church.

The fruits of this Revival were to be seen in the purifying of national sentiment, the sweeping away of slavery, and in the creation of a corporate conscience and a moral censorship that put an end to Government lotteries, and in the end freed public life from the venality and bribery that were rampant before it did its work. And the home life of the Evangelicals set the pattern of the pure home life that became the glory of England. But the spirit that sought to change the heart and renew the face of the homeland did not halt at its borders, and when it gathered strength, it launched forth on the high seas of modern missionary enterprise. Bible and Tract and Benevolent Societies of every kind owe their rise to its working, and what, by means of these things, the gospel has done is but an earnest of what it is fitted and destined to do in brighter and better days to come.

A GALAXY OF PREACHERS

How such a change, so fruitful in beneficent results, came about appears in the story of the worthies whose memory the godly Bishop of Liverpool, John Charles Ryle, has enshrined in his telling sketches. These appeared about half a century ago in the pages of the *Family Treasury*, and then, in collected form they were published as *Christian Life a Hundred Years Ago*, or *The Christian Leaders of Last Century*. In his vigorous, manly, downright style the Bishop gives in the story of Whitefield and the Wesleys, Walker of Truro and Hervey of Weston Favell, Rowlands of Llangeitho and Romaine of Blackfriars, Venn of Huddersfield and John Berridge of Everton, with their contemporaries and yokefellows. The writer was in thorough and outspoken sympathy with the men of whom he wrote, and he does not stint or grudge to give them the praise that was their due. And the lively and eminently readable account that he gives of these worthies of England is fitted to leave on the impressionable mind of youth the mark that the writer meant it to make. His enthusiasm for his heroes is catching.

BISHOP RYLE'S WRITINGS

Whatever is wanting in the writings of Bishop John Ryle, the note of definite conviction is not wanting, and it is positive conviction that is likely to beget positive conviction. An anaemic generation, nurtured on a bloodless theology, needs a tonic, and such a book as this supplies it. It puts iron in the blood. Let it be read and read again, and digested and assimilated. Those that have from its pages learned the work and worth of the men of whom it speaks will know what they stood for and what they did. It will stir them up to hold fast the truth of the gospel, and hold up its banner in the midst of all the declensions and apostasy of an age more remarkable for its lubricity and versatility than for its manly avowal of a Master who calls upon His servants to bear and to share His reproach.

The Lord God of Elijah lives, and when He gives a double portion of His spirit to a ministry that comes in the spirit and in the power of the prophet of fire, the hearts of the children will be turned to their fathers, and the disobedient will learn the wisdom of the just.

13: *Duncan Campbell of Kiltearn*[1], by Duncan Macgregor

The writer of this book was a lover of good men and a little bit of a hero-worshipper. These two things did not in the least stand in the way of his being a sympathetic and appreciative biographer. He loved and he admired the subject of his sketch, and so he threw his whole heart into his work when he essayed to tell who and what kind of man Duncan Campbell of Kiltearn was, and he had a ready pen to obey a willing heart.

Duncan Campbell was one of three remarkable brothers who were born in Roroyare in Glen Lyon.[2] Their lot was cast in days when Zion's King manifested His presence and His goings in the land, and all the three of them became His willing captives. David was the Disruption minister of Tarbat in Ross-shire, where he succeeded the godly William Forbes. To that parish he went from the Chapel of Ease in Inverness. He died minister of the Free Church of Lawers, thus closing his ministry in the district where he began it – his native Breadalbane. Patrick was not the least remarkable of the three. He remained in Glenlyon, where as teacher and leader in the congregation he wielded his great influence on the side of the Evangel. His elegy to the memory of his beloved pastor, John Macalister, is no mean specimen of the Gaelic sacred

[1]Kiltearn (the name of the parish of which Evanton is the main town) lies 9 miles South-West of Invergordon, in Easter Ross.
[2]Perthshire.

[76]

muse. Mr Macalister, whose son was the late Rev. D. M. Macalister of Buccleuch-Greyfriars Church, Edinburgh, was the first minister that the people of Glenlyon got for themselves, and he had the privilege and the responsibility of moulding them in their then plastic state. The Revival of Breadalbane[1] had deeply moved them, and they were as soft clay in the hands of a heaven-sent pastor. So great was the influence that he exercised, that years after he left the district it used to be said in Gaelic, 'Cha-ne laghan Bhictoria ach laghan Mhic-Alasdair a th' anns a' ghleann so.' (The laws of this Glen are not those of Victoria but those of Macalister.) Duncan Campbell was the other brother, and it happens that the account of his life is the most detailed narrative that we have of any of the family. It is now somewhat more than a hundred years since the great awakening of Lochtayside. It was not the first movement of its kind there, for a few years before, the preaching of one of the Haldane Itinerants, who afterwards went to America and on his way preached in Skye and left his mark there, had borne fruit in Breadalbane. There was, as the outcome of this movement under Farquharson's teaching, a leavening of Evangelical life in the community, and the active ministry of James Kennedy in the Independent Church of Aberfeldy kept the whole countryside from stagnation. This earlier movement, however, split into two rival sections, and lost much of its power largely through the dissensions among its followers on the question of baptism. But when Robert Findlater was appointed as missionary in Ardeonaig, sound solid definite Gospel teaching found a foothold in the Church of Scotland. It was at one of his Communions that the great awakening broke out under the preaching of Macdonald of Ferintosh, and the work was continued

[1] Amid Grampian Mountains of W. Perthshire.

under that of Robert Findlater and like-minded helpers like Donald MacGillivray of Strathfillan. The three brothers Campbell were fruits of this powerful awakening, and many others with them from Glenlyon and Lochtayside. In after years little bands of Evangelicals from those parts would make their way north to Communion services at Ferintosh or Redcastle. An old native of Glenlyon, the late Duncan Campbell, Editor of the *Northern Chronicle*, used to say that if one from Breadalbane were to be asked in pre-Disruption days who were the most eminent ministers in the Church of Scotland, the immediate answer would be Macdonald of Ferintosh and Kennedy of Redcastle.

'NO UNCERTAIN SOUND'

The warm Evangelical atmosphere that Duncan Campbell breathed in those years of blessing in Breadalbane he carried with him through life. He was settled at first in his native district, and along with his brother David he welcomed the visits of the Apostle of the North, whose daughter he afterwards married. A few years before the Disruption he was translated to the historic parish of Kiltearn, where for over thirty years he exercised an honoured ministry and revived the sacred traditions of the Gospel witness of Thomas Hog and William Stewart. There was no uncertain sound given by his trumpet, and in the stirring years that followed 1843 his labours were generously devoted to the service of the Free Church throughout the Highlands. He did not forget his native Perthshire, and from Lochaber to Lairg he was one of the most highly esteemed Evangelists of that Evangelical generation.

The task of recording the brief outline of his work could not have fallen into more suitable hands than those of

Duncan Macgregor. He too was a Breadalbane man brought up in the atmosphere of the Awakening. He was in full sympathy with the subject of his sketch, and in closest and most friendly touch with the whole circle in which he moved. In Stornoway, Glasgow, and Dundee, Duncan Macgregor was ever known as a warm-hearted Evangelical, and he was not in the way of hiding his light. His *Shepherd of Israel* lets one see what his own way of handling Christian life and work was, and his loving sketch, in an appendix to that work of his former neighbour, the saintly Robert Finlayson of Lochs, shows that his removal to occupy Robert McCheyne's pulpit in Dundee did nothing to cool the warm love that he cherished for the Disruption worthies of the North. McCheyne and William Burns had few faster friends than the fathers of the North. These fathers Duncan Macgregor loved, and he was loved by them in turn, and the fragrance of his love for them comes out in his references to them and their fellows and their predecessors, as he had occasion to mention them in telling the story of Campbell of Kiltearn.

'WHOSE FAITH FOLLOW'

This little book has now become very scarce, but in the districts and circles where it was bought and read it served to keep alive and green the memory of one of those worthies who spoke to their fellows the Word of God, and whose faith they might well follow even to the outgate of life. And the Christ that Duncan Campbell thus commended is the same to-day as He was yesterday, and what He was and is He will be for ever. It stirs the heart to refresh the memory in regard to those that were our fathers' leaders and guides, and as they followed hard after the Son of God be it ours in our turn to follow them as they followed Christ, and to transmit unimpaired to our successors the goodly heritage of gospel truth and living witness that they were honoured to hand down to us. If we are the legatees of our fathers we are trustees for our children.

14: William Wilberforce's *Practical View*

It is drawing near a century and a half since the name of
Wilberforce began to be well-known in the public life of
Great Britain. However prominent members of the family
have been in later years, they derive no small share of the
lustre of their name from the illustrious man whose book
we propose to notice. In a whimsical way he once wrote of
men of renown, reflecting according to Chinese ideas
credit on their ancestry who came to shine with post-
humous glory in the light diffused by their distinguished
descendants. However much interest the record of their
lives awakens in the history of their progenitors there is no
doubt at all as to the heritage such men leave to their
offspring. It may be that more is expected of them in
virtue of their lineage, but certainly their connections give
them great initial advantages as regards public interest
and favour in the race of life. On the other hand, as it has
been forcefully put, the pedestal on which they stand
proves to them a pillory if they show themselves unworthy
of the race from which they sprang.

The earlier generation of the Evangelical worthies of
eighteenth-century England was passing away when
William Wilberforce was in 1759 born at Hull. Hervey,
Walker of Truro, and Grimshaw had either run their race,
or were nearing the goal. Whitefield still lived, but in 1770
he finished his wonderful course. These men had their
successors,and the powerful Evangelical movement
which began about 1738 continued to swell in volume for

well nigh a century. In its earlier period it touched the fringe but only the fringe of the upper classes. Lady Huntingdon might say she was thankful that Paul wrote 'not many,' and not, 'not any,' when he said that not many mighty, not many noble were called. In the days of Cowper the movement could claim in the Earl of Dartmouth one that wore a coronet and prayed. But by the end of the eighteenth century the discovery of hidden danger that had long lurked unheeded in unbelief was made in connection with the upheaval of the French Revolution, and there was a beginning of reaction against the godlessness and infidelity that had long reigned supreme among the ruling classes. With this reaction came Wilberforce's opportunity.

In his youth, our author came for some time in touch with older Methodism in his aunt's house near London; but the seed that may then have been sown in his heart lay dormant for years. He enjoyed all the best advantages that a scion of the wealthy classes could command at the outset of life. Though his frame was feeble, yet his spirit was lively. He was endowed with rare charm of manner and disposition. His sweet voice and face and his unusual aptitude for public work and speech, brought him as the pet of fortune to the place of influence that he learned so well to fill. The youthful and the life-long friend of the younger Pitt, he secured a seat in Parliament as representing his native county of York, and his gifts soon won for him the ear of his fellow-senators. But more was in store for him than the fading laurels of earth's glory.

WILBERFORCE'S CONVERSION

About the age of twenty-five he went on a Continental tour with a Cambridge don, who was afterwards Master of

Queen's College and Dean of Carlisle. This was Isaac Milner, the brother of his old master in Hull, Joseph Milner. This companion already had Evangelical leanings, but they had not yet crystallised from sentiments into convictions. There was, however, a striving on foot that produced momentous results. The two young men took with them as a travelling companion Doddridge *On the Rise and Progress of Religion in the Soul,*[1] and, as leisure afforded opportunities, they read this work and searched the Scriptures to see whether its teachings were those of the Prophets and Apostles or not. From this study the youthful statesman derived life-long profit. The whole current of his being ran in a new channel, and he had in due time the honourable calling to take over the succession to the godly Sir Richard Hill as a Christian witness in the Hall of Parliament, while his wealth and his generosity to good causes brought him into touch with such princely givers as the Thorntons. The darling of society became now the associate and loved companion of the Evangelical witnesses who had borne the brunt of the battle. The veteran John Newton took him to his heart. Richard Cecil, Charles Simeon, Henry and John Venn, became his comrades, and the cause of the Evangel became the dominating interest of his activities. Hannah More and her sisters were at work in the West of England teaching the poor and ignorant, and showing how consecrated womanhood can devote itself to the raising of the submerged tenth. Hannah's tract, *The Shepherd of Salisbury Plain*, is still remembered. It was, however, only one of many that she wrote. These efforts engaged the sympathetic interest of the brilliant legislator. The era was that from which the great Missionary, Tract and Bible Socie-

---

[1] It was published in 1745. In 1736 both Aberdeen universities had recognised Doddridge's services as a preacher by presenting him with the degree of Doctor of Divinity.

ties date their beginning, and Wilberforce threw himself heart and soul into such good causes. But the work of his public life with which his name will ever be associated was his warfare on Slavery and the Slave Trade.

ABOLITION OF SLAVE TRADE (1807) AND SLAVERY (1833)

Even in his boyhood his mind was turned to sympathise with the victims of violence and oppression. But when the iron of Christian resolution entered into his blood he gave himself to the task of fighting a vested interest that had become a national reproach. With like-minded fellows, Clarkson and Buxton and our Scottish Charles Grant, and Macaulay, he carried on his war, and ere his eye was closed in death he knew of the triumph of the cause. This leaven of Christianity, which wrought in British public life, threw off the incubus of an accursed system. And it did more to elevate and to purify the tone of national sentiment and to reflect lasting glory upon our land and race than a thousand Trafalgars and Waterloos. If Lady Blessington, with her charm, was said to lay on the whites whom she made her slaves those chains from which Wilberforce freed the blacks, the epigram that puts this on record sets forth what is the glory of the Parliamentary life of William Wilberforce.

In the last decade of the eighteenth century, when he was about thirty-eight years old, Wilberforce published his *Practical View*. In it he surveys the life of professing Christendom in the light of what professing Christian truth calls for. With candour and faithfulness he lays bare to view the inconsistency between profession and obligation on the one side and faith and life on the other. The book is temperate, courteous, and studiously restrained in its language. It is the work of a man of affairs who was not a man of the world, and the position, popularity, and authority of the writer commanded an audience. It soon told on the life of England, and with its amiable spirit and winsome tone it influenced the educated and the upper classes. James Hervey had, in the style which the culture of his day favoured, written to commend the Gospel to the cultured classes. But here was a work which flowed from no professional pen, and which, free from the suspicion of clerical bias, carried with it the token and hall-mark of its own sincerity. The impetus that it gave to practical religion continued for many a day, and the remote ripples and wavelets of its influence are still to be detected upon the surface of the sea of mankind.

PRACTICAL VIEW: ITS DIRECT EFFECTS

Of the direct effects produced by this work we shall mention but two. The one was the conversion of Leigh Richmond. A generation has arisen that knows little of this gracious servant of Christ. But his tracts, such as *The Dairyman's Daughter*, still live. They are not forgotten. Richmond did noble work in his day in connection with the works of the Reformers and Modern Missions, and one of the most affecting things we have read in Evangelical biography is his sketch in *Domestic Portraiture* of the life and death of his son, Wilberforce. This godly youth was named after the writer to whom his father owed his own self, even his very soul. The other effect that stands out in memory is the conversion of Thomas Chalmers. What that stood for Scotland had reason to know, and the world well knew it. Should there be nothing more to show that Wilberforce did not write in vain, this would furnish us with abundance of proof. Thus a chain goes back from Thomas Chalmers to William Wilberforce, to Philip Doddridge, to Richard Baxter, to Richard Sibbes. Along the links of that chain by pen and in life the power of the Spirit of God is to be seen.[1]

[1]LINKS IN THE CHAIN
from *17th Century to 19th Century*.
RICHARD SIBBES:
The Bruised Reed (1630)
↓
RICHARD BAXTER

'It pleased God that a poor pedlar came to the door . . . and my Father bought of him Sibb's *Bruised Reed* . . . It suited my state . . . and gave me a livelier apprehension of the mystery of redemption and how much I was beholden to Jesus Christ . . . Without any means but books was God pleased to resolve me for Himself'.

In 1657 Baxter's *Call to the Unconverted* was published. Many years later it was blessed to the conversion of
↓
PHILIP DODDRIDGE:

whose *Rise and Progress of Religion in the Soul*, printed in 1745, was used to bring into the light of God the soul of
↓
WILLIAM WILBERFORCE:

whose *Practical View of the prevailing Religious System of Professed Christians . . . contrasted with Real Christianity*, published in 1797, helped to bring from death into light and life the soul of
↓
THOMAS CHALMERS

who wrote: 'Somewhere about the year 1811 I had Wilberforce's *View* put into my hands, and as I got on in reading it I felt myself on the eve of a great revolution in all my opinions of Christianity. I am now most thoroughly of opinion . . . that on the system of "Do this and live" no peace . . . can ever be attained. It is, "Believe on the Lord Jesus Christ and thou shalt be saved".'

15: Thomas Jones' *Life of Lady Glenorchy*

The righteous shall be had in everlasting remembrance. Even on earth this memory does not die out. Sometimes, however, a name is familiar more to the ear than to the understanding, and many have heard the name of Lady Glenorchy who have but the haziest idea of who she was. There must have been many who bore the title, for it is the courtesy title of the heir of Breadalbane's[1] lady. Yet among the many there is one name that stands out so clearly that when people speak of Lady Glenorchy only one is thought of among the holders of the title in the past. The possession of the title in any single generation might give a certain standing to the Lady Glenorchy of the day. But when their days of wearing this title were over, they were no longer known by it, and the name of the godly viscountess held the field as the Lady Glenorchy of all time. Names and titles ennoble many. She ennobled her name and title.

This she did by a life record of self-sacrifice and Christian service. She did not live long. Before the years of old age came upon her she was taken home to her rest. But from the time that she was called by grace, she lived the life of a fruitful branch in the True Vine. While still in the flush of youth and beauty she became the captive of the gospel and the bond-slave of Christ Jesus. Her position of prominence in the ranks of the Scottish aristocracy made it hard for her to tread the narrow path. At home she

[1]Part of Perthshire

might have met with more sympathy than fell to her lot, and outside it meant that she must share the reproach of Christ if she publicly connected herself with movements aiming at the advancement of His cause. There was, however, a godly circle in the upper classes of Scottish society, so that when she joined herself to the Lord and to His people she was not altogether without comrades in enduring reproach. The evangelical traditions of the Sutherland family were by this time fading away. The Reays were still evangelical, Lady Maxwell was even Wesleyan, but the centre of gospel witness among the titled class was the Leven family – the old and staunch friends of Whitefield. The Breadalbanes had been more Whig and Protestant than evangelical. Now, however, when Willielma (her surname was changed to Campbell when her widowed mother re-married) Maxwell, Lady Glenorchy, espoused the cause of the Evangel, in the midst of all the reproach it met with, the most forceful personality that the upper classes furnished as a recruit to the good cause was enlisted. She was forceful, however, not as a hustler, but as a moral and spiritual force, and one that possessed initiative and did what in her lay to leave her country better than she found it.

In this kind of work she had a contemporary who did similar work in England. It was the era of Selina, the godly Countess of Huntingdon. These great ladies were of one heart and soul. But Lady Huntingdon possessed a virile character that was in marked contrast with the shrinking unobtrusiveness of her Scottish friend. Kindred spirits drew to each other, and at Bath, then the great watering place of fashionable England, Lady Glenorchy came in touch with that section of English society that was leavened with gospel sympathies. Her bosom friend was Jane Hill, whose remarkable brothers, Sir Richard and Rowland, were two of the most outstanding evangelists of their day. Miss Hill was at once a Christian and a theologian, and one might look far before finding finer gospel letters than those she addressed to her Scottish friend. The *Life of Lady Glenorchy*, by her minister, Dr Thomas Jones, gives a number of them. The friends of Jesus, though few in their class of life, were warm, and perhaps their very fewness and the greatness of the reproach they had to bear for His name, made them more to each other.

LABOURS IN VARIETY

In Scotland Moderatism was at its zenith. Yet there were living witnesses not only among the Seceders and Relief[1] but in the Church of Scotland. Indeed, on both sides of the Moray Firth the bright day of gospel power was on, and the names of the worthies of those days are not yet forgotten in the north – Porteous and Fraser of Alness, Hector Macphail and James Calder. The last of these, the saintly minister of Ardersier and Croy, was one of her ladyship's correspondents, and one can see from his diary as published how highly he esteemed her. The separation of sympathy that afterwards took place between northern and southern evangelists had not yet come about. There was much to do in the Highlands both of Perthshire and further north, and in this connection Lady Glenorchy was not idle. She got the godly son of her living correspondent – John Calder – as minister of Weem in her own country, whence he went north afterwards to Rosskeen. She was busy getting Gaelic literature diffused, and as Kilbrandon

---

[1]Seceders: those who opposed the intrusion of unsuitable ministers, and, led by the Erskine brothers, withdrew from the Church of Scotland in 1733.

Relief: In 1761 Thomas Gillespie and others formed the Relief (Presbyterian) Church in protest against the action of 'patrons' who compelled congregations to accept ministers of whom they did not approve.

was on the Breadalbane estates, she got John Smith, afterwards of Campbeltown, who was then minister there, to put his fine Celtic scholarship at her disposal in the translation of Joseph Alleine's *Alarm to the Unconverted*. As he advanced with the work, he used what he translated as pulpit matter, and when the people of Kilbrandon came thus in touch with the bones of the Puritan prophet, an awakening began, the memory of which has not yet passed away.

THOMAS JONES & OTHERS

Further south she was diligent in furthering the evangel-isation of the lapsing or lapsed masses, and her name is still borne by the Church in Edinburgh that represents the congregation which was gathered to her chapel. Lady Glenorchy's Church was long a centre of holy evangelical activity.[1] Thomas Jones, who became its minister, was a rigorous Welsh Calvinist. He became as Scottish as half a century in Scotland's capital could make him, and in this connection he became one of the Scottish evangelists that set their faces against the admission to the praise of the sanctuary of any material save the Psalms of inspiration. His bosom friend was John Colquhoun of Leith, and in this matter their sentiments coincided. The family of the Bonars was but one of the many evangelical families connected with his congregation, and Dr Begg began his public work as the popular assistant of Dr Jones in his latter years.

Dr Jones' *Life of Lady Glenorchy*[2] is a book for edification. It is rich with gospel sentiment and spiritual experience, and it will interest those that would acquaint

---

[1] She also built chapels at Carlisle, Matlock, and Strathfillan (on the Breadalbane territory).

[2] She lived from 1741 to 1786.

themselves with the worthies of our past. John Eastman and Robert Walker, John Gillies and Robert Balfour of Glasgow, were among her ladyship's set, and the maintenance of a warm evangelical witness in the dark days of the Moderate ascendancy was much helped by her self-denying efforts. Her race, as we have said, was early over, but her memory, enshrined in Dr Jones' life, is one of the abiding treasures of Scotland's religious history.

16: Thomas Scott's *The Force of Truth*

There are few more interesting narratives of conversion of the quieter order than that given by Thomas Scott in his *Force of Truth*. Brought up to work on the land, he had early ambitions, and the grit that was called for to give them effect. And the methods adopted by the Church of England, taken in conjunction with the culpable laxity of her administration, afforded him the opportunity of achieving a successful issue.

Throughout the eighteenth century the secular sentiment that pervaded the upper ecclesiastical ranks found fit expression in non-residence of the clergy and in pluralities. This called for a host of curates to do duty in what would otherwise have been vacant charges, and to meet the needs of the situation the standard of admission to the ministry was low. Thus it came about that a Church, which in its higher reaches attained a reputable standard of learning, had a large number of ministers whose qualifications were of a very elementary character indeed. And in this state of things it was no hard task for Thomas Scott to secure ordination.

His early advantages were not great, but he was bookishly inclined, and disposed to be very positive in maintaining the opinions he had espoused. His views of divine truth were worse than defective. They were definitely and dangerously erroneous. But the Church, whose Articles were Calvinistic, and whose clergy were Arminian, allowed a sufficient latitude to permit one who had got beyond Arminianism and was decidedly Socinian to serve in her pulpits.

UNBELIEF & APOSTASY

By the end of the third quarter of the century the depths of Socinian apostasy from the Evangel had been sounded, and just as this scarcely veiled unbelief had wrought havoc in the old Nonconforming Churches, there were found men in the Anglican Church who were ready not only to get rid of the confession of Evangelical truth, but also to proclaim to the world their definite disavowal of it.

The same cold breath of unbelief that blighted the life of religion in England withered a large section of the Church of Scotland. For the 'Moderates,' as they called themselves, who were the dominating party in her courts, were not only to a large extent Socinian in their tendency, they were scheming to get away from the obligation that they had of their own accord undertaken of acknowledging the old Reformed and Puritan standards as the Confession of their faith. And before the end of the century they did not shrink from giving expression in the most public form to the negative theology that they adopted and entertained.

Theophilus Lindsey, and a few of the bolder spirits of the party in the Church of England, went the full length in avowing their unbelief of the cardinal verities of the Evangel, and became professed Socinians. But they left behind them sympathisers who were not prepared to take the plunge. Of these were men like Thomas Scott when he started his ministerial life. But for Scott there was better in store. In the providence of God the sphere of work assigned to him brought him into the neighbourhood of good John Newton.

[93]

JOHN NEWTON OF OLNEY (BUCKS.)

John Newton of Olney was the leading representative in his district of a class that were everywhere spoken against. He was an avowed Calvinist, and to be that put him beneath contempt in the judgment of those who were swayed by the spirit of the age. And to begin with, Scott, like the rest of his fellows, looked down on his neighbour as an enthusiast. But the two came in contact. At first Scott was markedly opinionative and arrogant. Avoiding everything that was fitted to irritate, Newton was firm and kind in defending his own convictions and in dealing with his militant antagonist, and step by step that antagonist was led on in the knowledge of Scripture truth until, in the end, he became a preacher and defender of the faith that he had once derided and destroyed. The narrative of his course of study, inquiry, and prayer is given in the little work of which we write. It is a plain and unvarnished tale of the leadings of the Spirit of God, which brought the writer to the knowledge and the acknowledgment of the Reformed Faith, of which he had been for some years a professed but unprofitable teacher. For the rest of his life he was to be the theologian and expositor of the evangelical school in his Church, and as such he stood in a righteous relation to the 39 Articles of Religion.

At the outset of his public life he accepted the sophistical reasoning that was current in regard to creed subscription. But there was a strain of blunt honesty in his composition, and it was on this that Newton fastened and worked. Scott had a sound natural judgment, and with his studious habits he made up for his early handicap. To the end he continued to be a student, and no amount of toil would keep him from facing the task to which he heard the voice of duty calling him. Thus, at the age of sixty, he set about the acquisition of Arabic, that he might be useful in advancing the cause of the Gospel in connection with new openings that presented themselves.

DEFENDER OF THE FAITH

As a preacher and letter-writer and genial human companion Scott was always behind his father in the faith. But his sturdy integrity and common sense made his teaching valued by those that had discernment. And in his day, in the midst of difficulties from broken health and impaired finance, there was no more manly, consistent, and upright defender of the faith in his country. Sir James Stephen, who knew the 'Clapham Sect,' as they were called, gave a place to Thomas Scott second to no man of his time. He was indeed one of the great doctors[1] of the Church of England, and how he came to be what he was is set forth in the account he gave of his experience in the *Force of Truth*.

The same truth that he came to learn and prize has suffered an eclipse in the Reformed Churches of our time more grievous than that which overtook it even in the eighteenth century. But the same Lord who raised up witnesses in dark days, and gave His blessing with their word of witness, can again turn the battle to the gate; and our young folk and old folk alike might get good from acquainting themselves with the memorial of God's gracious dealings with one of the fathers of the Evangelical movement, while those who have read it before might be all the better for renewing their acquaintance with a work that is not forgotten, though now well-nigh a century and a half has passed since the events occurred and the inquiry took place that the book records.[2]

[1] In 1807 a college in Carlisle, Pennsylvania, gave him the degree of Doctor of Divinity. It was completely unsolicited and he never used it.

[2] *The Force of Truth* has been reprinted recently by the Banner of Truth.

17: Charles Hodge's *The Way of Life*

In the mid-nineteenth century it was said that the outstanding men of the Presbyterian world were Thomas Chalmers, Henry Cooke,[1] and Charles Hodge. Hodge was then in his prime. Indeed he was not quite fifty when he was thus put along with the two leading men in the Reformed Church in Scotland and in Ireland as one of the first three among the mighties of that evangelical age of his denomination.

Charles Hodge was a native of Philadelphia, where he was brought up in a circle that cherished the memory and the teaching of George Whitefield. The great Methodist evangelist finished his course in America, and his influence told mightily on various branches of the Protestant Church. The congregation of which the Hodges were members was set on foot to furnish a spiritual home and a nursery for the Presbyterians of Philadelphia who sympathised with the Great Revival. And they and those that thought with them introduced into the American Presbyterian Church the strain of Methodism that put it out of touch in the matter of worship with the older traditions of Reformed Christendom.

The earnest Christian spirit that breathed in the circle in which his early years were spent was not without its influence on Charles Hodge. When he was still but young, his godly widowed mother, for the education of her sons,

[1]1788–1868: a strenuous defender of orthodoxy in Ulster.

took up house in Princeton. Here in his college days her husband had studied and graduated in the days of President Witherspoon, and with this home of American Presbyterianism her distinguished son was to be associated through his long life. In turn his sons and his grandson are also associated with it. And this long connection has given rise to the Princeton puzzle, 'What is Princeton?' with its answer, 'An everlasting prossession of the Hodges and the Alexanders.'

When Dr Archibald Alexander, the patriarch of his renowned name, was settled as the first professor in the newly opened Theological Seminary of Princeton, Charles Hodge was but a boy of fourteen still at school, and preparing for college. He was a witness of the induction of that Gamaliel at whose feet he was himself to sit and whose work he was to carry on to an even higher pitch of success than attended the labours of his master. Shortly after Dr Alexander came to Princeton, there was a wonderful work of grace in the College as the fruit of his preaching, and of that of Dr Ashbel Green, the pastor of Charles Hodge's youth, who was now the President of Princeton College. Many of the men who were to be, in after years, in the forefront of evangelical life in the States came then under the power of the gospel. It is to this time that Hodge's definite conversion belongs. He was almost the firstfruits of the movement.

At the close of his theological curriculum Hodge was appointed, largely through the influence of Dr Alexander, as one of the professors in the new theological seminary. Here he began his life work. A few years later he spent a year or two in Germany to acquaint himself at first hand with the scholarship, the faith, and the unbelief of that country. On his return unscathed to his home he pursued the even tenor of his way, and down to the end of his life in 1878 he was a professor in the famous seminary in which he had been trained. Much of the fame that Princeton has won was through his academic and literary work. In due course he succeeded Dr Alexander, with whom he lived as a son with his father. Between them they filled the chair of Systematic Theology for two-thirds of a century, and Princeton became celebrated in the old world as in the new as the home of the Theology of the Reformation and the Westminster Confession.

Hodge was the defender and the expositor in his day of old and pure Calvinism. He was a man of wonderful lucidity of thought, who had a gift of expressing his clear thought in equally clear speech. His warm heart and tender feelings went side by side with his clear head to make him as attractive an exponent of the faith of the Reformation as the nineteenth century saw. He was much in controversy, but for all that the irenic prevailed over the polemic in his nature, and few men were more lovely or beloved than he.

HODGE & CUNNINGHAM

Dr Kennedy of Dingwell visited America in 1873, and on his return he is reported to have said that there were two things he saw there that exceeded his expectation, and these were Niagara and Dr Hodge. In the days of the great Principal Cunningham, one of his students consulted him as to whether if he took a session at Princeton it would count as one of his course. The Principal expressed a doubt on the matter, but the doubt he expressed was whether a session taken under Hodge should not count as two instead of one. Hodge and Cunningham, the protagonists of the Reformed Theology on the two sides of the

Atlantic, were like two brothers. Each looked on the other as the foremost theologian of his day. Hodge the exegete was a master of commentators. Hodge the theologian was a master of divines. Hodge the churchman was a master of ecclesiastics. But our present concern is with a little book that he produced in the department of practical and personal religion.

THE WAY OF LIFE

The Way of Life was written at the invitation of an interdenominational body, the American Sunday School Union. Without at all hiding his light the writer sets forth the way of life in a most attractive style. The work was written to meet the needs of intelligent, educated young men. But what with the author's pacific temper, his clear thought, and his limpid purity of style, it was heartily accepted by the S. S. Union Board as a handbook for the rising youth of various churches. Before it was printed, Archibald Alexander, who saw it in manuscript, was afraid that it was too definite in its doctrinal utterances to meet such wide acceptance. The welcome, however, that it met with tells a heartening tale as to the soundness of judgment that characterised the evangelical churches of America eighty years ago. What this little book was fitted to do when first it saw the light it is fitted to do still.[1] A more winsome presentation of cardinal Christian truth it would be hard to find. The learned divine was a skilful evangelist.

[1] This splendid book has been reprinted by the Banner of Truth in paperback form.

18: John Kennedy's *The Apostle of the North*

The memory of the just is blessed, and the fragrance of such a memory cleaves to the name of John Macdonald of Ferintosh.[1] There was no one man that did more than he to evangelise the Highlands of Scotland. Born in Caithness, the son of the excellent James Macdonald, Catechist of Reay, he breathed an atmosphere that was saturated with warm gospel influences from his very childhood. A vigorous evangelical life flourished in the eighteenth century in Northern and Eastern Sutherland, and in the Gaelic part of Caithness, and no finer specimen could be found in those parts of the fruits of the Gospel than James Macdonald. As a Christian he was as remarkable for his graces as for his gifts, and his zeal and sanity of judgment kept pace.

From his infancy the Catechist's son, John, was a bright boy, able to learn anything he tried, and full of life and humour. He went forward to the university, however, still a stranger to the power of the gospel, with the letter of which he had such opportunities of being familiar. But during his college course John Macdonald was arrested by the grace of God. In those days Mr Robertson of Kingussie was missionary in the Heights of Caithness, and his warm and powerful preaching was blessed to the future 'Apostle of the North.' At the same time John

[1] 1779–1849. Ferintosh is a hamlet in Ross and Cromarty not far from Cononbridge and Dingwall.

Macdonald came under the spell of the master mind of Jonathan Edwards, and from this time forward he aspired to serve the Lord in the work of the ministry.

At the university Dr Macdonald took a high place. It is said that he was never lower than third in any of his classes. He excelled in mathematics, and mathematics continued to be one of his favourite studies to the end of his life. When he wished to whet the edge of his mental powers he was wont to tackle a difficult mathematical problem, and having solved it he found his faculties in working order for attacking any other mental work that called for his attention. In this respect he resembled quite a number of his Disruption fellows – Chalmers, Gordon, Forbes were outstanding mathematicians in their day. And among their post-Disruption successors, Hugh Martin and John Kennedy of Dingwall walked in their steps. Our fathers and leaders in the Evangel were no weaklings. Their unusual powers of mind found their chosen field of exercise in the most excellent knowledge of all.

'IN LABOURS MORE ABUNDANT'

After a short apprenticeship in the charge of Berriedale, Dr Macdonald became minister of the Gaelic Church of Edinburgh, and here he got his wings. When he reached the age of 33 he was settled as successor to the saintly Charles Calder in the parish of Ferintosh, and this parish was his home for the remaining thirty-six years of his life. Ross-shire was highly favoured in its evangelical ministry, and he found himself in a congenial circle. But though his home was at Ferintosh, it was only the centre of the circle. As the door of opportunity opened Dr Macdonald availed himself of it, and such demands were made on his time that he spent hardly more than half the year in his own parish. From St Kilda to Breadalbane he had almost the whole Highlands as his parish. And in different places where he preached there was a remarkable outpouring of the Holy Ghost. This was the case not only in the Islands – Skye, Lewis, Harris, and St Kilda – but also on the mainland from Sutherland to Lochtayside. In labours he was more abundant than others, and his labour was not in vain.

Possessed of a strong and vigorous constitution, a man of middle height and strong build, he was cut out for a life of hard work, and such a life he had. There has likely been no one in the ministry in Scotland that preached more than he did. He had a voice of wonderful compass and power, and, highly musical as he was, he could manage it perfectly. And when he preached, people gathered. It has been said that none of the old chiefs ever wielded such authority among his countrymen, and it might well be said, for his countrymen never had a more sane and healthy influence at work among them than they had in his ministry.

GAELIC POETRY

Along with his other endowments Dr Macdonald was richly endowed as a bard. It is true that his Gaelic poetry is largely didactic in substance and elegiac in form. But much of it is poetry of pure quality and high finish. He had the North Country gift of pithy expression, and many of his terms are very happy. Among his elegies are those on Charles Calder, his predecessor; Dr Stewart of Dingwall, his beloved neighbour; and John Kennedy of Redcastle, his brother and yoke-fellow in the gospel. But the two best of them were his elegy on his father in the faith, Mr Robertson of Kingussie; and his threefold elegy on his own worthy father, James Macdonald of Reay. This last is perhaps the best-known and oftenest quoted of all his poems, and we do not know anywhere a better account of the old godliness of the North Highlands than it affords. He sang also of the work of the Spirit of God in His people, and of St Kilda. In the generation that is past there were few pieces of Gaelic poetry that were better known throughout the Highlands and among the scattered children of the Gael in Canada and Australia than the poems of Dr Macdonald. To estimate the place he won in the heart of his countrymen one would need to mix with the Highland settlers in Canada who in his days went overseas. Among them his name was the outstanding one of their old Highland life, and his poems were a link with the past and the home they had left behind.

THE APOSTLE OF THE NORTH

Dr Macdonald was happy in his biographer. The mantle that fell from him as he went home alighted in a pre-eminent degree on the son of his great comrade in the gospel, Kennedy of Redcastle; and John Kennedy of Dingwall, who entered so richly into his labours, wrote his life. The high culture and the marked style that character-ised anything to which he put his hand appears in this work, and we could wish nothing better in its way for our young folk than that they should read Dr Kennedy's *The Apostle of the North*. It is the life of an evangelical giant written by another. And that the memory may be perpetuated of the great days of the past when the goings of the Lord were seen in His sanctuary,[1] we should treasure this work as one of our favourite friends. If you have not got it, search for it, borrow it, read it, and, when you have done so, you will know with what good reason it has been recommended to you.

[1] Psalm 68:24.

19: W. K. Tweedie's *Life of John Macdonald of Calcutta*

Sixty years ago the works of Dr W. K. Tweedie of Edinburgh[1] had a public of their own. They commended themselves as healthy home literature to heads of households, with definite evangelical convictions. Nowadays they are almost forgotten. But one of his works should not be. It should live not only or so much for what there is in it of William King Tweedie, but also and much more for what it tells of John Macdonald of Calcutta. This missionary-minister made a profound impression on the men of his day.

John Macdonald belonged to a race that was highly favoured. For generations his ancestors were conspicuous not only for their parts, but even more for their piety. The son of John Macdonald, of Ferintosh, the Apostle of the North, and the grandson of James Macdonald, the Catechist of Reay, the Christian whose praise on his way to Jordan, on its brink, and over the river, his famous son sang in memorable Gaelic verse, John was surrounded with the kindly influences of godliness from the outset of life. In his early years he showed his prowess in the academic arena, and bade fair to leave his mark on his age as one of its very ablest men. But when the kindly arrest of the gospel salvation was laid upon him, he gave himself up without reserve to the work of the holy ministry.

[1]Pastor of the Free Tolbooth church.

John Macdonald is one of the saints of the Church in Scotland. The old Christians of Ross-shire, who were devoted to his father, could speak of that father's eminence. But those of them that knew the son found that words failed them to set forth his excellence. And this estimate of his Christian character and whole-hearted devotedness to his Lord was one that was shared by those that came within the circle of his acquaintance wherever he went. He must have been a remarkably holy man.

Dr Kennedy, of Dingwall, could say of the father in conversation that he was the most honoured by his Master of all the fathers that he knew, and at the same time that he was the lowliest. When he uttered this judgment, he was asked if there was any special cross in his lot that kept him down and left him so humble. His answer was: 'That is not how I explain his wonderful humility at all. I ascribe it to the sense that he had of the freeness of the grace of the gospel.' Yet to say the least, John, the son, did not fall one whit behind such a father.

Years after John Macdonald's death, the godly John Milne, who left Perth to take up the work of the Calcutta charge of the Free Church of Scotland, and who was a lover of good men, sought eagerly for all the information he could gather about the sainted missionary whose life had appealed to him before he left Scotland. And he used to tell with appreciation the remark made about John Macdonald as he lay unconscious on his death-bed. Among the many friends who visited the sick-room was the veteran Swiss missionary, Lacroix. As he looked at his dying friend, he said, 'There lies the holiest man in India.'[1]

---

[1]Horatius Bonar in his *Life of Rev. John Milne* speaks of John Macdonald as 'that noble missionary who in his brief course, gave such a decided testimony for Christ in Calcutta and shone there as a burning and shining light' (p.227).

At an early age the future missionary was ordained to the gospel ministry in one of the London charges of the Church of Scotland. In the great metropolis the elective affinities of the hidden life drew him to men like-minded with himself, and the drawing was reciprocal. James Harrington Evans was then exercising his richly blessed ministry in London, and senior though he was to the young Scotsman, he was one of his set. In seeking the society of such a man, John Macdonald showed where his heart was. But the appreciation that he had for his older friend serves to indicate how rare a specimen of the man of God Harrington Evans was. For whatever John Macdonald was he was out and out, and the chosen companions of such a man have their encomium in the very fact that they have been so chosen.

SERVICE IN CALCUTTA BEGINS

In those London years of well-nigh a century ago the leaven of the gospel was working mightily in the life of the Church. And on his return from Calcutta the meteoric triumphant Home Campaign of Alexander Duff bore fruit in awakening a missionary interest throughout the congregations of the Church of his fathers. He did not go back to India without recruits, and among them was the young Scots minister from London. It was not without searchings of heart and searching of the Word of God and seeking of counsel from the Lord Himself that John Macdonald offered himself for missionary service in India. His Statement of Reasons for coming to the conclusion to which he came is published, and it reveals the deep spirituality and the thorough godliness of the writer.

Some time after he went to Calcutta he published *A Pastor's Memorial*, which gives a taste of what his high-toned preaching was. He was a Richard Baxter over again, only a Richard Baxter free from aberrations. In this volume, which does not often turn up, the Statement of Reasons is reprinted. The discourses in the *Memorial* might well serve as a model for youthful preachers. They are the work of a man who was on fire with zeal for God's glory and love to men's souls. These discourses, and a few of his tracts, are the surviving memorials of his consecrated life and work. The tracts are such as 'The Suffering Saviour.' 'Shall I go to the Theatre?' 'Shall I go to the Ball?' Along with these there is a choice little book that the missionary minister edited. It was the manuscript of Isobel Hood of Elgin.

Isobel Hood's manuscript is one of the choice pieces of living experimental divinity. It shows how the powerful preaching of Dr Ronald Bayne reflected itself in the life of a lowly one among his hearers in the Little Kirk of Elgin. The editor was in full sympathy with his work. And the earnestness that yearned over the salvation of the land of his chosen work found utterance in his appeal to his readers to 'Pray for India.'

MACDONALD THE PREACHER

In Calcutta John Macdonald made his mark. He was the outstanding and outspoken witness of his day, and European society felt his presence. He was not afraid to lift up his voice and cry. The Evangel that his father preached with power was his Evangel too. Thomas Chalmers once had the opportunity of hearing the father, and as he went home from the service, he remarked to his companion, 'I understand the secret of Macdonald's power. He preaches Justification by Faith'. This held, too, of his like-minded son.

Anyone that wishes to know more of Macdonald of Calcutta will find that Dr Tweedie's pages enshrine the memory of a life that we should not willingly let die. John

Macdonald, at the age of forty, finished his course.[1] Thus he predeceased his eminent father by two years. And few more touching funeral sermons have been preached than that delivered by the bereaved father when he got the news of his death. 'It is well.' It was well that he was born, well that he was educated, better that he was born again; well that he entered the ministry, well that he went to India. And now, at last, it was well that he died. Being dead he yet speaks.

[1] 1807–1847.

20: Duncan Macfarlan's *Revivals of the 18th Century*

In the years that followed the Disruption of 1843, there was a Publications' Scheme in the Free Church of Scotland which gave wide and cheap circulation to books that were fitted to interest, instruct, and do good. Lovers of our Reformation Theology might thus get select writings of Dickson or Rutherford, of Traill or Willison. Lovers of the godly lives of our old worthies got the life of Halyburton or of Mrs Veitch and Thomas Hog, and M'Crie's sketches of the lives of Henderson and Guthrie. A selection also from the works of our great Reformer was given. And in this goodly series along with others of like kind there was published Duncan Macfarlan's work on the *Revivals of the Eighteenth Century*, chiefly that of Cambuslang. The writer was the Disruption minister of Renfrew.

DUNCAN MACFARLAN

In his early life he was brought up in a congregation of the Relief Church.[1] But in his college days he came under the wonderful influence that was wielded by Chalmers in his Glasgow ministry, and from the Relief he came over to the mother Church of Scotland which was then awaking out of the sleep of fashionable unbelief. To the end of his life Dr

[1] See footnote 1 (Ch.15 p.89).

Macfarlan followed closely in the steps of his venerated teacher, and represented that enlightened Evangelicalism which was so widely diffused in the reforming Church of pre-Disruption years, and which prepared her for her stand on behalf of the Evangelical principles of her Constitution which called for the Disruption. This was its crowning protest against a loose Erastianism which at its cold heart had no love for the old gospel, which gospel, by its loyal adherence to the glory of Christ in His three-fold mediatorial office determined the history and contendings of our fathers in Reformation and post-Reformation days.

Duncan Macfarlan's first settlement in the ministry was in succession to the great and godly Dr Love in the Anderston Chapel of Ease, Glasgow. After a short ministry there he was admitted to the parish of Renfrew. In this town he continued to labour until his death, as parish minister and afterwards as Free Church minister. The fact that the Anderston congregation called him in his youth was an index to his whereabouts. Throughout life he was the strenuous defender of the Evangelical verities, and in two departments in particular his zeal distinguished itself. These two were eminently characteristic of our older Scottish Evangelism, the defence of the Lord's Day and his steady interest in the progress of the work of the Gospel. He lived in reviving times. They were the times that brought about the Disruption. They made it possible. And the ministers who led the Evangelical Revival were, as Dr Warfield well remarked, the representatives or the spiritual successors of the Puritans of the seventeenth century, who did more than any others to elaborate and illustrate the doctrine of the work of the Holy Spirit of God. After Dr Macfarlan's death his *Life* was written by his neighbour and friend Dr Smith, of Lochwinnoch, with whose daughters in later years Eliza Fletcher was in close touch. The *Life* is not well-known. But to appreciate fully our Disruption Fathers one must know of Duncan Macfarlan and the place that he held and filled. He made his own distinct contribution to the work of his age. For he was by no means the least among the mighties. At an early stage in the history of the Free Church he showed the manliness of one who was not prepared blindly to accept the dictated policy of headquarters.

LINKS WITH NORTH AMERICA

Dr Macfarlan's work makes no claims to special literary merit unless it be, and indeed it is, an excellence that a writer should say succinctly and clearly what he has to say. He begins by glancing at the blight and deadness that came over the Reformed Churches on both sides of the Atlantic in the early years of the eighteenth century. He takes notice, too, of the steps taken by the gospel's well-wishers to advance its cause. The first remarkable awakenings took place beyond the Atlantic. One of the earliest of these was at Freehold in New Jersey under the preaching of John Tennent in 1730. The remote outcome of this work may be said to be the Presbyterian Church in the United States of America. It is linked in a curious way with the history of the suffering Church of Scotland. Among those who were banished in the killing times was a young man, Walter Ker. He remained in New Jersey, and his fellows who came back to Scotland bore witness to his zeal and earnestness. Before he was exiled, as his acquaintance Patrick Walker tells us, he lived near Lanark with an aged couple who were the fruit of the Monday service at the Kirk of Shotts in 1630. A century after, in 1730, Walter Ker was happy to see work of a like kind in his district of New Jersey. It was he who was mainly responsible for getting John Tennent as minister at

Freehold, and after bringing him there he was a tower of strength to him in the work of his short ministry. But the most noted of the transatlantic awakenings of the earlier period was that which took place under the preaching of Edwards at Northampton. His observant eye took note of it, and his sane judgment comes out in the narrative that his pen has left of it. On these earlier movements, however, he does little more than touch.

WHITEFIELD AND THE WORK IN CAMBUSLANG

Dr Macfarlan soon comes to the home field and tells of the awakenings that were in Scotland in the years following 1740. These were not confined to Cambuslang and Kilsyth, though these were the chief centres. As far north as Golspie and Rogart and Nigg the quickening of the Church extended. The beginning of the Cambuslang work took place under the preaching of William M'Culloch, the minister of the parish. But the great awakening occurred at a Communion season under the devoted George Whitefield, who was at the time a young man of less than thirty. In those times on Communion occasions neighbouring churches were shut and their congregations flocked to the scene of the Communion. Concurrent services within the Church and outside were held, and every effort was made to reach the crowds with the word of the gospel. This was part of the old order, and however it was liable to be abused it lent itself to the possibility of great good. During the Cambuslang work Mr M'Culloch was assisted by a number of the best Gospel preachers in the south of Scotland. Among these, to name no more, was as a chief helper his neighbour in Glasgow, that Evangelical giant John M'Laurin. No name would carry more weight than his in his generation. There were two men of the period whose mental build resembles his, the one was the masterly reasoner, Joseph Butler of Durham, the other was the great divine of New England, Jonathan Edwards. No man in Scotland was less likely than he to be swept off his feet by a wave of emotional enthusiasm. 'Zeal warmed his breast and Reason cooled his head.' And he gave whole-hearted support to the work. Among the hearers there was one well-fitted to judge, and in his *Life* we have a glimpse of Cambuslang. This was Dugald Buchanan, who in after days was to be the catechist of Rannoch.

Embodied in Dr Macfarlan's narrative we have much material that he drew from information that was at the disposal of the M'Culloch family. Janet M'Culloch of Dairsie, the widow of Robert Coutts, the young minister of Brechin, was one of the inner circle of Dr Chalmers' intimates. She gave the family papers bearing on the great awakening in her grandfather's days to the library of the Free Church College. There was also a *Monthly History* of the work of God at home and abroad, published at Glasgow, on which he drew as contemporary evidence in regard to the awakenings. Dr Gillies of Glasgow, who wrote the *Life of Whitefield* (and who was the son-in-law of John M'Laurin), embodied large portions of this *History* in his Historical Collections[1]. These Collections found a sympathetic editor for their second edition in Horatius Bonar of Kelso in Disruption days. This work is a storehouse of information bearing on awakenings, whether Puritan or Evangelical, whether of the Reformation, the century of the Covenants or the eighteenth century. Evangelicalism, with a good back-bone of definite convictions and outspoken witness on behalf of the gospel, tells its tale in his pages. What is relevant for his period to the Scottish situation is taken up by Dr Macfarlan.

[1]Republished in 1981 by the Banner of Truth.

THE 'BLINK OF REVIVAL'

If the Kirk of Shotts prepared a crop of Christians in Clydesdale to be Christ's witnesses in the dark days of the Covenanting struggle, the blink of revival in the fifth decade of the eighteenth century made ready a seed of witness who were to stand for the truth in the darkest days of Moderatism, days of flagrant unbelief. Indeed, that blink is perhaps the brightest spot in the religious history of much of the North of Scotland. It showed what a heaven-sent revival is and can do. Our times, and the decayed state of Evangelical witness and life, call aloud for another mighty revival of the work of God. 'Awake, awake, put on strength, O arm of the Lord, awake as in the ancient times in the generations of old.'

21: William Carus' *Memoirs of the Life of Charles Simeon*

Charles Simeon left his mark deep on his generation. The Church of England felt and still feels the results of his work. Before the end of his life he wielded an influence in the Christian world that was hardly less than that of the whole Bench of Bishops. One of such power could be no ordinary man. Nor was he. As far as natural endowments go he did not rise much above mediocrity. But he traded with his two talents and they brought in a full return. Not so much great native ability as great holiness and single-eyed devotedness to the glory of God characterised him, and behind him his Master's steps were to be heard. The record of a life such as his is one that is worth having. His work went far to leaven the Church of England with evangelical sentiment. He was at the head-waters of so many of the collective activities of the modern world, that it is of decided interest to see who and what the man was.

The Biography that tells his life story is not, by any means, an exciting narrative. It was meant to be not so much a tale of deeds as a volume gathering together papers and furnishing sufficient material to bind them into a unity. The biographer was in thorough sympathy with his subject. But he wrought within the bounds of restrictions imposed by Mr Simeon and accepted by himself. The bulky volume of the earlier editions was afterwards reduced in size. For those who wish to have in brief compass the facts of Simeon's life and work there is a short biography and estimate by the late Bishop of Durham, Dr H. C. G. Moule. The full work, however, by Canon Carus is invaluable for the faithful presentation which it gives of the convictions, sentiments, trials, and triumphs of the great evangelical leader.[1]

CONVERSION AND LIFE WORK

Simeon belonged to the higher classes of society. Born at Reading in 1759, he was educated at Eton, and from Eton passed to King's College, Cambridge, which became his headquarters for life. Shortly after he went to College he found that he must attend the Lord's Supper in about three weeks' time. This discovery was the occasion of his awakening, for he thought that the devil himself was as fit for taking part in that service as he felt himself to be. In his early religious life he had no friendly hand to guide him. But One higher than man had him in hand. He read that the Jews knew well what they did when they laid their hand on the head of the sacrifice. Light broke in on his troubled conscience. He was enabled as 'an Israelite indeed' to lay his hand on the head of the Lamb of God as his Sacrifice. Thus he found peace and was brought to rejoice in his Lord who had been delivered for his offences, and was now raised again for his justification. The decisive bent was given to his life.

That life was destined to be eminently a University one. In due course he became a fellow of his College – King's – and his rooms there were his bachelor home until his death. Shortly after his ordination he found a field of work in Trinity Church, Cambridge, and in spite of long and bitter opposition, he succeeded in making his pulpit

[1]Canon Carus was Fellow and Senior Dean of Trinity College and minister of Trinity Church, Cambridge. Simeon died in 1836. The First Edition of the *Memoirs* appeared in 1846.

influence felt by town and gown. While still a young man he came in contact with John Wesley, and the *Life* gives an interesting conversation that the two had in which the irenic triumphed over the polemic. Henry Venn, too, the old friend of Whitefield and Lady Huntingdon, of John Berridge and Rowland Hill, came to Yelling, which is hardly more than an easy afternoon's ride from Cambridge. Here the health which was shattered by his Herculean work in Huddersfield was recruited, and Simeon and many other young evangelicals from the University town came in touch with one of the ablest, honest, and most devoted of all the fathers of the Evangelical Revival. Simeon owed him much.

In the later decades of the eighteenth century, the reactionary policy of the authorities of the Church of England forced things to a head. All that stood for Methodism outside the parochial system, or that interfered with what were held to be the rights of the Incumbents of parishes, was refused a standing ground in connection with the State Church. Thus Methodism alike in its Calvinistic and in its Arminian form was extruded. Lady Huntingdon's Connexion and the Wesleyans had to organise their work as tolerated movements outside the Church Establishment. This policy resulted in a certain exclusiveness on the part of the Evangelicals in the Church. They were cut off, except such incorrigibles as John Berridge and Rowland Hill, from the friendly and brotherly intercourse which they had formerly enjoyed with their fellow-believers who were not of the Church of England. This policy embittered the Dissenters, and in the end contributed largely to their political agitation for Dis-establishment. The outlook of the Evangelicals within the Church became narrower. If the circumscription of their activities did this, it did something else too. It impelled them to more concentrated effort in the field that was still left to them, and to make the most of every opportunity they had of entering where a door opened before them in their own communion. Simeon, more than the earlier leaders of the Revival movement, restricted himself to the narrower sphere that was thus at his disposal.

VISITS TO THE HIGHLANDS

Before he worked off the zeal of his early days, he came to know many of the Evangelicals of Scotland who held up the banner of the gospel during the Moderate eclipse. On one of his tours to Scotland, the record of which is left out of the third edition of his life, Simeon came as far north as Tain, and was on the most friendly terms with the Calders and Angus Mackintosh. Indeed, he preached more than once for Charles Calder in Ferintosh on week-days, and hundreds of hearers gathered to hear English preaching so early in the Black Isle, preaching normally being in Gaelic at this time. Hugh Calder of Croy was his host and guide while he was in northern parts. On one of his visits to Scotland he spent a night in the Manse of Moulin. This was an eventful night. It was the turning-point in the life of Alexander Stewart, the minister of the parish. Afterwards known as Dr Stewart, the author of a masterly Gaelic grammar and reviser of the translation of the Gaelic Bible, he became the minister in succession of Dingwall and of the Canongate Parish in Edinburgh. Before he left Moulin for his Ross-shire charge he was richly blessed in his ministry at Moulin, and the remote results of Simeon's call at the Manse were found in the life and work of Dr Alexander Duff. The great Indian missionary was a native of Moulin and was the son of parents whose Christian life was the fruit of the Gospel preached by Alexander Stewart.

MISSIONARY INFLUENCE

This was not the only link by any means that bound the Fellow of King's to the spread of the gospel in India. Through his friend, Charles Grant, who ruled India from Leadenhall Street, the influence of Simeon told on the appointment of chaplains in the service of the East India Company. Brown, Corrie, Thomason, Buchanan are names that mean much in the early efforts to evangelise India. Above and beyond them all was Henry Martyn. Those all were of Simeon's set, and Martyn in particular, the Senior Wrangler and fine scholar of his year at Cambridge, owed to Simeon his very soul. In the early days of the great religious societies, Simeon was in the forefront in promoting their work and defending their aims. The C. M. S. reckons him as one of its fathers and founders. So, too, the London Jews' Society. He stood by his friend Wilberforce in his campaign for Negro Emancipation. And the Bible and Tract Societies felt his helping hand.

At length, for years before his sun set, he who at the beginning of his career was looked on as a pariah or outcast in the religious life of Cambridge and the Church of England, came to be looked up to as a kind of patriarch. The leaven of the Methodism which wrought in his early days remained with him to the end. It was congenial to its Anglican origin and to an Anglican environment. In so far as its principle diverged from that of historical Puritanism, it accounted for the attitude which he took up on some important questions when these two principles came into conflict. In these things, such as the circulation of the Bible without the Apocrypha, we have no doubt that the Puritan was the more single-eyed policy, and its results have justified it. Apart, however, from those things in which the friends of the Evangel did not see eye to eye,

Simeon stood for what was best in the life of England in his day, and he remains in his life and work a monument of what the consecration of the two talents to the service and glory of God is fitted to do.

22: The *Works* of John Maclaurin

After the death of Thomas Halyburton in 1712, perhaps the finest mind of the Church of Scotland in the first half of the eighteenth century was that of John Maclaurin. His brother Colin was the most eminent mathematician that Britain produced in his age. He became the expositor of the *Principia* of Isaac Newton in Edinburgh, and did much in his own subject to raise the reputation and the standard of attainment in his native country. But eminent as he was for his mental endowments he was at least equalled by his brother John, born five years before him. Their father and their uncle were ministers in Cowal after the Revolution Settlement. They held the two contiguous parishes of Kilmodan or Glendaruel and Kilfinan. John, the minister of Kilmodan, died while still a young man and his brother Daniel brought up his boys at Kilfinan. In completing his theological course the elder of the two brothers took a session at Leyden. The Netherlands were just past their meridian glory in theological learning and soundness but they were still the home of the Theology of the Reformation. A session or two at Utrecht or Leyden or Francquier or Groningen was no uncommon crown to the curriculum of the youthful aspirants to the ministry in the Scottish Church. In the years of persecution our fathers were in close touch with Holland as the asylum for the refugees. And the fashion of studying in the famous Dutch Theological schools kept the ministry in Scotland abreast of and alive to the discussions of the Schools of

Continental Europe. This helped the Church to recover from the severe handicap that the repressing policy of the Stuarts imposed on the thorough equipment of the Presbyterian ministry in Scotland. Men of John Maclaurin's build of mind were fitted to derive special benefit from a thorough course of study.

In the early years of the restored Presbyterian Church, the Synod of Argyll, before it came under the blight of 'Moderatism' and unbelief, was the Synod that did most to knit the Gaelic-speaking Highlands to the rest of Scotland. Its ministers were indefatigable in translating the Psalter, the Catechisms, and the Confession of Faith into Gaelic, and the father of John Maclaurin took his own share in this work. He read for the Press the proofs of the Synod's metrical version of the Psalms. The hereditary jurisdiction of the Argyll family counted for much in the Western Highlands in those days. And such men as Boes of Campbeltown and Daniel Campbell of Glassary showed in their teaching and work how their life was saturated with the faith of the Reformers. It was in a circle that knew this warm breath that John Maclaurin spent his early years, and when he entered on the work of the ministry there was no mistake as to the colours that he carried.

MINISTRY IN LUSS

Maclaurin's ministry began at Luss on the banks of Loch Lomond in the year 1719. That same year his uncle Daniel, who had brought him up, was translated from Kilfinan to Rosneath so that uncle and nephew were neighbours. After four years in Luss, John Maclaurin, now in his thirtieth year, was translated to the old Ramshorn Kirk in Glasgow, which was known as the North-west or St David's Church. In this charge he did his life-work. Until his death in 1754 he was a central figure in the lively evangelical society that was found in the capital of the West. He took a leading, helping part in the services at Cambuslang during the great awakening there. He corresponded with brethren in New England, especially with Edwards, who shared his great interests. It was in a letter from him to Edwards that the suggestion was thrown out which bore fruit in the Concert of prayer for the reviving of the work of God. The help given to Edwards from Scotland while he was impoverished after the break from his church at Northampton, Massachusetts, was largely owing to Maclaurin's exertions. In many respects Maclaurin resembled Edwards. Both were men of profound intellect and of equally profound spirituality Maclaurin had indeed been spoken of as the Bishop Butler of the Scottish Church. His massive powers were like those of his two great contemporaries.

AN EVANGELICAL

Specimens of ecclesiastical flotsam have ventured to speak of Maclaurin as inclining towards 'Moderatism.' Nothing could be further from the truth. He might speak of moderate men of his own way of thought. But the word moderate has a good meaning of its own that does not need to be confounded with 'Moderate.' There were many among the orthodox men who were moderate or temperate, and others of them who tended to be rabid or extreme. Their opponents called the whole school of the Evangelicals the High-fliers, a nickname that belonged properly only to a section of them. Yet as the difference of 'Moderate' and Evangelical became accentuated, 'Moderatism' scouted or shunned the mysteries of the Faith and left even the temperate statement and proclamation of them to those that were not afraid of the reproach of the Gospel. Fashionable 'Moderatism' aspired to a reputation for culture and good breeding, and fled as it would from the plague from anything so vulgar as what commended itself to the common herd. It acted as though the representatives of the Evangel were but weaker brethren that had to be put up with. The fact was that such men as John Maclaurin, John Witherspoon and John Erskine were men of the most masculine understanding and of the finest culture that Scotland could show in the eighteenth century.

ESSAYS AND SERMONS

When the descendants of the Seceders began to be less exclusive and one-sided, if at the same time less definite, in their theological thought, the third in the succession of the three John Browns edited and prefaced a volume of Maclaurin's *Essays and Sermons* and recognised in him 'the most profound and eloquent Scottish theologian of the eighteenth century'. The *Essays and Sermons* were published in 1755, the year after the author's death. His work on the Messianic Prophecies was given to the world in 1773 by his son-in-law, Dr John Gillies, the biographer of George Whitefield. The American Presbyterian Board of Publication published a transatlantic edition of the *Essays and Sermons*. But the complete edition of Maclaurin's work is in two volumes and was edited during last century by Dr W. H. Goold. The discourse on *Glorying in the Cross of Christ* has been often printed and much admired. Dr R. S. Candlish spoke of it in glowing terms as the finest evangelical sermon that he knew. John Macrae of Knockbain and Greenock, speaking to the late Mr Cameron of Back, said that since he had read Maclaurin's sermon he had never ventured to preach from that text. This discourse had appeared in beautiful Gaelic. The translator was Dugald Macphail, the Mull bard who used to be one of the elders of Hope Street Free Church, Glasgow. Only less celebrated than this is Maclaurin's sermon on *The Sins of Men not chargeable to God*. Another choice piece that has been reprinted is his discussion of *Prejudices against the Gospel*. This, with a similar piece by Dr John Inglis, was published by that good Free Churchman and fine divine, Dr James Buchanan.

Maclaurin from his cast of mind was never fitted to be a preacher specially popular with the thoughtless crowd. A thoughtful and exercised audience would appreciate him. For the serious reader who will patiently think out his thoughts there are scarcely any names on our Roll of Honour that stand higher than his. In the years of his ministry at Luss he was a preacher of Gaelic, and in later years, with the inflow of many Highlanders into Glasgow, he led the way in preaching to them in their own tongue just as his contemporary Gael in Edinburgh, Neil Macvicar, broke like ground in his own city.

These titles, described in the book, are currently available:

THE CHRISTIAN'S GREAT INTEREST
William Guthrie

Describes in a clear and attractive style what it means to be a Christian, and how to become one. Its author, William Guthrie, was described by John Owen as 'one of the greatest divines that ever wrote'.

CHRISTIAN LEADERS OF THE 18th CENTURY
J. C. Ryle

The best introduction to the 18th century and undoubtedly Ryle's finest piece of historical writing. Contains vivid biographies of the men who 'shook England from one end to the other'.

THE FORCE OF TRUTH
Thomas Scott

This once famous best-seller presents the testimony of a man who struggled to show his parishioners their need, but was unable to point them to any answer until he himself yielded to the claims of Jesus Christ and 'the force of truth'. Thomas Scott (1747–1821) was a friend of William Carey.

LETTERS OF SAMUEL RUTHERFORD
Edited by Andrew A. Bonar

'What a wealth of spiritual ravishment we have here! Rutherford is beyond all praise of men. Like a strong-winged eagle he soars into the highest heaven and with unblenched eye he looks into the mystery of love divine.'

C. H. SPURGEON

THE WAY OF LIFE
Charles Hodge

As a popular and devotional work this was Hodge's master-piece. Deals with Scripture, Sin, Justification, Faith, Holy Living, etc.